Working with Hannah

Working with Hannah is a unique and detailed snapshot of the first years of schooling for a child with Down's syndrome and severe mobility and communication problems. Written by two classroom assistants who supported Hannah during her two and a half years in a mainsteam infants school, this book shows how the right level of support can make inclusion a success not only for the child and family but also for the school itself. The book is written in a practical way and describes the 'hands-on' approach of Hannah's day-to-day management in a busy school. It covers:

- finding a school
- how the school prepares
- adapting the curriculum
- recognising the importance of friendship
- incorporating therapies into the school day
- additional aspects of personal and physical care
- setting up communication systems.

There are key points at the end of each chapter which summarise the ways in which to approach providing the various types of support.

Working with Hannah details an extraordinary experience and gives the reader the unique opportunity to follow the very human story of Hannah's inclusion. It is an important book which gives classroom support assistants, teachers and SENCOs the confidence to tackle inclusion head on. Parents of children with varying degrees of learning difficulty will also find this account both encouraging and informative.

Before working as classroom assistants for children with special educational needs **Liz Wise** worked in marketing and PR before becoming a counsellor and **Chris Glass** had a background in nursing and nurse education.

Working with Hannah

A special girl in a mainstream school

Liz Wise and Chris Glass

London and New York

First published 2000
by RoutledgeFalmer
11 New Fetter Lane, London EC4P 4EE

Simultaneously published in the USA and Canada
by RoutledgeFalmer
29 West 35th Street, New York, NY 10001

RoutledgeFalmer is an imprint of the Taylor & Francis Group

© 2000 Liz Wise and Chris Glass

Typeset in Goudy by Wearset, Boldon, Tyne and Wear
Printed and bound in Great Britain by TJ International Ltd, Padstow, Cornwall

British Library Cataloguing in Publication Data
A catalogue record for this book is available from the British Library

Library of Congress Cataloging-in-Publication Data

Wise, Liz, 1955-
   Working with Hannah: a special girl in a mainstream school / Liz Wise and
Chris Glass
      p. cm
Includes bibliographical references.
ISBN 0-415-22282-6
   1. Mentally handicapped children – Education (Early childhood) – Great Britain – Case
studies. 2. Mainstreaming in education – Great Britain – Case studies. 3. Inclusive
education – Great Britain – Case studies. 4. Down's syndrome – Great Britain – Case studies.
I. Glass, Chris, 1950- II. Title.

LC4636.G7 W57 2000
371.95'2–dc21   00-030591

To
Hannah

and to

Colin, Caroline, Anna and Olivia

Andrew and Emily
and
George Glass (1917–2000)

Contents

Acknowledgements

We would like to thank Hannah's parents, Alayne and Michael Levy, for so generously and unconditionally sharing Hannah's story with us. Also Hannah's brothers Ari, Noah, Yonni and Yoel (the latest addition) who, together with their parents, make up this exceptional family.

We thank Lynne Thompson, Head teacher at Trafalgar Infant School, Pat Richards, Tricia Robinson and Sue Small, Hannah's class teachers, and all the staff at the school. Helena Chambers, her specialist teacher, provided the expertise in the area of Hannah's day-to-day learning and recording procedures that proved so effective. Laura Prendergast, Hannah's close friend, and her mother Eileen, and Linda Hicks, Hannah's Brownie leader, also made valuable contributions to this book.

We thank Sue Strudwick, Chris Hughes and Claire Leighton for their advice and support, and Barbara Mistry for so selflessly sharing her own experiences of having a child with special needs.

This leads us on to Madeline Harrison, class and music teacher at Trafalgar Infant School, who is best known for her expertise in making music such an important part of the school day. Her multi-talented skills include art, and we thank her for the illustrations she produced for this book. A special thank you goes to Sally Krajl, Special Needs Co-ordinator, for her encouragement, enthusiasm and for teaching us so much. Jo Power, a parent-governor, gave us a huge amount of her time and support in reading through our book and making valuable suggestions and corrections which pointed us in the right direction.

We would like to thank all our friends and numerous family members who supported us through our writing and never seemed to mind that they didn't receive birthday cards or phone calls, and lunch and supper invitations were never reciprocated.

And finally we must not forget our families.

Liz thanks her husband Colin, whose constant support, advice and encouragement helped to make this book happen, and her three daughters Caroline, Anna and Olivia for being supportive and for the gentle reminders that there was life beyond writing.

Chris thanks her husband Andrew for putting up with the volatile moods, the dust and the out-of-date food, and her daughter Emily for forgiving those inevitable slips, like forgetting to collect her from athletics.

The following organisations contributed to Hannah's life in school and the writing of this book:

The Makaton Vocabulary Development Project, the Down Syndrome Educational Trust, the Centre for Micro-Assisted Communication, the Down's Syndrome Association, RM Window Box (the trade marks RM and RM Window Box are owned by Research Machines plc ane are used with their kind permission), Oxford University Press, Hazel Mill Toys, Blu-Tack, a registered trademark of Bostik Ltd, and The Project for Children with Special Needs based in Richmond, Surrey.

Preface

This book is about Hannah. She is an unusual child who, despite having severe learning and physical disabilities, was educated in a mainstream infant school. We, the co-authors, provided her with one-to-one support in the classroom during that period, on a job-share basis.

As Hannah moved on to her junior school we talked at length about what we had learned from our time with her. It was an extraordinary experience. We had periods of anxiety and uncertainty, particularly at the beginning, and times of intense elation and reward. We want to pass on some of our experiences to others who are concerned with the inclusive education of children with special needs.

We begin with a brief background to the education of children with different types of disability. We then outline the stages many parents go through to ensure the best education for their child. The remainder of the book tells Hannah's story. We shared the writing and within each section the use of the word 'I' emphasises our individual contribution.

Working with Hannah reveals some intimate details of the day-to-day life she experienced in school. We discussed the book with Hannah's parents and have their approval to share some very personal experiences. We also spoke to Hannah about the details we were including in her book. As the physical aspects of care can be the stumbling block when including children with physical disability, we felt it was important not to skip over these but to tackle them head on. By doing so we hope to remove any of the mystique surrounding them and describe, in a very practical way, how we dealt with the problems that arose.

Our account shows the benefits of including a child with severe learning difficulty into mainstream infant education. Hannah's experience was unique and came about through a variety of circumstances. We are aware that there are parents of many similar children who are unable to secure anything near such a high level of support. Their child, therefore, has not had the same opportunity for inclusion into mainstream schooling.

We hope that this book acts as a catalyst for change in the traditional thinking that children with severe learning difficulties cannot be accommodated in mainstream education. Given the right level of support, the whole school community benefits. The parents of all children with severe learning disabilities can take great encouragement from Hannah's story. She was truly inspirational and showed us all what can be achieved.

1 An overview of inclusive education

There have always been children with different types of disability in our society. At the beginning of the twentieth century, depending on the nature and severity of the disability, a child could spend a large amount of the time in a hospital or institution or, if lucky, be cared for at home. For many of these children, the experience of going to school was not an available option. For those with a mild disability, or one that had gone unnoticed, they might get to school and be taught alongside other children. Record books from the time use such terms as 'imbecile', 'cretin' and 'weakling' to describe those children who found it hard to 'keep up' with their peers.

When considering disability, the model used until recently was one of a deficit or problem that lay within the child from a medical or psychological point of view. The 1944 Education Act defined categories of disability with, in addition, a group that was deemed to be uneducable. These categories included blindness, deafness, physical impairment, speech problems, educational sub-normality and maladjustment. Special schools were set up to educate these groups of children. In 1970 the law was changed, and there had to be provision for the education of all children with disability. Responsibility for this new initiative moved from health authorities to education authorities, and no one was deemed to be uneducable.

The Warnock Report (1978) was a watershed in the approach to the education of children and young people with disability. There was a move away from the medical/psychological model that presented learning difficulties as fixed within the child. Instead, they put forward a model that emphasised the dynamic nature of learning and focused on the specific needs of the child within the home and the learning environment. It was recognised that the home background, the way the child was educated and the curriculum delivered were of paramount importance in determining the learning that took place. The term 'learning difficulty' was proposed, divided into the categories of mild, moderate, severe and specific. It was pointed out that these children had 'special educational needs' that were not that different from some of their peers in mainstream education.

The 1981 Education Act took up many of the Warnock Committee's recommendations. It gave a definition of special educational need as 'a learning difficulty which calls for special educational provision to be made ... significantly greater than [that] of their peers of the same age', or 'those with a disability that impedes access to education'. Local Education Authorities were required to ensure that children with these special educational needs were educated in mainstream schools provided that:

- the views of parents were taken into account
- the school could combine the special provision for the child with the education of other pupils
- there was efficient use of resources.

The Education Act (1993) (subsequently consolidated into the 1996 Education Act) introduced the Code of Practice offering practical guidance for schools and education authorities with regard to the education of children with special needs. Schools were required to identify a Special Needs Co-ordinator (SENCO) with the responsibility of ensuring that the school adhered to the special educational needs policy and that the Code of Practice was implemented. This is outlined in more detail in Chapter 2.

The legislative framework was in place. Disability rights groups and bodies such as the Independent Panel For Special Educational Advice (IPSEA) were instrumental in helping to change the climate so that children with learning difficulties were seen as children first and foremost; the role of the school was to provide the learning opportunities best suited to that child. Despite this philosophy, there remained a great deal of anxiety in ordinary schools with regard to meeting the needs of these children. There could still be the tendency to separate many of them out into special schools or adjoining 'units'. Many classroom teachers and head teachers remained unsure of their ability to cope with children with special educational needs and to meet their day-to-day learning requirements. Because of this, there has been a new emphasis on providing training and support for staff. Teacher training courses now have special needs education as an essential part of their curriculum. There are many very useful publications, notably from David Fulton Publishers, to inform and enhance the work of the teachers. There is also a National Association for Special Educational Needs which produces relevant journals and is dedicated to improving the development of children and young people with special educational needs and to supporting those who work with them. Despite these developments, governors, teaching staff and often local education authorities can remain apprehensive when including these children in mainstream schools. More training and support is becoming available but, at times, remains patchy and hard to access.

This book has been written in order to demystify the experience of having a child with severe learning difficulty and extreme physical impairment in a mainstream school. It describes the day-to-day needs of a specific child and how these were met within the ordinary school environment. Problems did arise but were overcome. We hope that by sharing the experience and offering approaches and practical solutions which we found helpful, we will give parents and teachers the confidence to include more children with significant learning difficulty and/or physical problems in mainstream schools.

2 The statementing process

The realisation that a baby is different and may have a range of disabilities is the beginning of a long and hard struggle to ensure the best for that child. Some parents know from birth that their child is going to have long-term problems. If the diagnosis is obvious, they will be told very soon after the child is born. This is a critical time, and the manner in which they are told can have a lasting effect on the parents' attitude and response to their child's disabilities. Parents remember forever how the news was 'broken' to them, how supportive the professionals were and what underlying message was being delivered.

Perhaps it is even harder for parents who do not have a clear diagnosis from the beginning. They watch their child failing to thrive, not meeting the milestones reached by peers. The baby is seen by a myriad of professionals – midwife, GP, health visitor, hospital doctors, community paediatricians. Parents clutch at straws – friends and family reassure them:

* 'Lots of babies roll their eyes.'
* 'My niece's child was slow to gain weight and she's fine now.'
* 'My feeling is that he will grow out of this and catch up with the others.'

There comes a time when there has to be some sort of realisation that the child *is* different. That first indication can come as an enormous shock. It may be in the form of a chance remark from one of the many professionals seeing the child: 'Of course this type of play is typical in children with autism.'

Parents who have lived with a niggling fear for months or years now have to face the reality of having a child with disability. At this time they have to cope with different authorities and professionals, all there to help the child but with their own political, financial and professional agendas. Parents have to find their way through the numerous bodies and agencies who are supposedly available to them and yet who seem steeped in red tape, employing a language which maybe totally alien to them.

* 'Is he on the special needs register?'
* 'Has she been having Portage?'
* 'Have you asked for a statement yet?'

Knowing that a child has long-term disabilities, parents are faced with a journey which is completely different to the one they envisaged. They may be unprepared and frightened. They slowly accumulate a huge amount of information regarding their child's physical health, speech, social skills and fine and gross motor techniques. In addition they and their family have to make decisions while finding their way through new systems, cultures and politics. All this at a time when they are acutely aware of the need to do the 'best' for their child, who is already at a disadvantage.

A child with a disability may become known to the authorities in several different ways. From birth they may be placed on the local authority register for special educational needs. This is to help with long-term planning of resources required in the area. Some areas may have 'Portage' support available. This service originated in a place called Portage in Wisconsin, North America. It involves working with children of pre-school age in their own homes and monitoring their progress in the development of speech, gross and fine motor skills and social interaction. If a child is receiving Portage at home they will become known to the school psychology support service. The Local Educational Authority (LEA) is then alerted that the child may require some sort of extra support when they reach school age. During these years other professionals may become involved with the child: physiotherapist, occupational therapist, speech therapist, dietician, health visitor, GP, community paediatrician, hospital specialists, educational psychologist, clinical psychologist. The list can be daunting for parents trying to formulate priorities for their child.

In addition to these professionals in mainstream care, parents will be faced with many other approaches and suggestions regarding what is best for their child. Cranial osteopathy (see glossary), aromatherapy massage, 'brushing', special diets, could all be offered as suggestions. Parents have to decide the best way of helping their child. They will slowly build relationships with the professionals involved and may have the help of a partnership worker who can support and enable them in their communication with different bodies/professionals.

Children born with a disability may require formal support in their education and this is outlined in a 'statement'. The statementing process itself is set out in 1993 Education Act. The *Code of Practice on the identification and assessment of special educational needs* (Department for Education 1994) followed the Act and was to give practical advice to parents, local education authorities and the governing bodies of maintained schools. It included monitoring arrangements for children with special needs, guidelines for parents and the setting up of special educational need (SEN) tribunals to offer a quick and independent system of appeal against decisions about which parents are unhappy. The code offered a five-stage assessment process to assist the education of children with special needs. It is important to realise that a child may miss some stages, and that the process may not even begin until after the child has attended school for the first time. Not all children will move up through the stages to a statement; the formal assessment procedures which may lead to statementing only begin at Stage 4. Children can move down through the stages as well as up.

Alternatively, the health or social services department may have brought pre-school children to the attention of the Local Education Authority, or the parents may have made a formal request themselves.

Stages 1 to 3 of the statementing process are school based and do not require the statutory involvement of the Local Education Authority (although the educational psychologist may be called in at Stage 3)

Stage 1

This stage takes place when there is an expression of concern from the class teacher that a child is showing special educational need, together with some evidence for that concern from another teacher, parent or another professional. At this stage the teacher would seek advice from the Special Educational Needs Co-ordinator (SENCO) in the school and consult the child's parents. The Head teacher may be informed.

The class teacher is responsible for gathering information to make an assessment of the child's special need and, usually with the help of the SENCO, initiate different work in the classroom to better meet the needs of the child. The teacher will also monitor and review the child's progress with the parents, usually at the Parents' Evening. The SENCO ensures the child is included in the school's SEN register.

Stage 2

The SENCO takes the lead in assessing the child's learning difficulty and planning, monitoring and reviewing the provision. The child's parents are kept informed and an individual education plan (IEP) is formulated for the child. The trigger for this stage may be a review of progress at Stage 1, or the SENCO may start a child on Stage 2 if early intensive support is deemed necessary.

Stage 3

The school calls upon external specialist support usually following two reviews at Stage 2; or if the SENCO considers early intensive action, with outside support, is necessary. The school may first call upon a special advisory teacher from the LEA, followed, if necessary, by an educational psychologist. If the child's needs are complex, the referral could go straight to the educational psychologist. The child may receive additional specialist support from the LEA at this stage, for example for hearing or visual impairment, behavioural or specific learning difficulties.

Nationally, in almost three per cent of children overall, the Authority will have to make a statutory assessment of special educational need. This happens when it appears that the child's needs may not be met within the normal provision available in the school.

There is statutory involvement of the LEA at Stages 4 and 5.

Stage 4

The Authority is asked to consider the need for a statutory assessment of the child's special educational needs. The referral may come from the school, or parents may formally request it themselves at any stage. It is important to realise that statutory assessment does not always lead to a 'statement'. The information gathered may indicate that the child's needs can be met within the school without any provision determined by the LEA.

The LEA must write to parents informing them of their proposal to make a statutory assessment. If parents wish to submit their own written evidence they are asked to do so within 29 days. The parents are given access to a named officer in the Authority and a named person (independent of the Authority but knowledgeable in these matters) to help them in the whole process. When making a statutory assessment, the LEA seeks parental, educational, medical and psychological views of the child and may ask for a report from social services.

Within ten weeks the Special Needs Panel of the Authority meets to assess the child and must decide whether or not a statement is necessary to meet his or her educational needs. If the Authority decides not to make a statement, it must within two weeks issue a 'note in lieu' of a statement, setting out the reasons for the conclusions and telling the parents of their right to appeal. This document is then available to those who work with the child to help them meet his or her educational needs.

Stage 5

This involves the issuing of a statement. Should the LEA decide to make a statement, drafting the proposed statement should take no more than two weeks. This is issued to parents with a notice setting out the arrangements for the choice of school, the parents' right to make representations about the content of the statement and their right to appeal. The final statement, with the agreement of the parents, should be completed within eight weeks.

The type and amount of support the child requires will be outlined in the statement. Once this is finalised it is legally binding to the education authority. They are bound to provide what is written in the statement or the parents can challenge them through the tribunal system.

It is up to the school to review the statement annually when progress and future targets are discussed. This ensures that it continues to meet the child's educational needs.

Relationships and trust are of paramount importance in the process of writing the statement. Parents must feel that the interests of their child are being met. The Education Authority, on the other hand, must ensure that it is able to make the most efficient use of resources. Meeting this one child's needs must be compatible with the interests of other children in the area.

Perhaps the most stressful time for parents is Stage 4, the assessment process itself. The Authority collects reports from all those involved in assessing the educational needs of the child. Those writing reports may include therapists, medical practitioners, social workers and playgroup leaders. There will also be a report from the educational psychologist who will assess the child and summarise his or her educational needs. When all the reports are collated, parents read for the first time how these professionals see their child. This can be a very stressful time. It may seem as if the child and the family are being judged.

A written report from the parents can be a vital part of this process. Parents can outline the particular needs of their child and make representation in favour of a particular school. This can be a difficult task. Parents are aware that their report is contributing to the final level of support the child will receive. Did they stress the right areas of concern? Could they have worded it differently and been more forceful? Were they too demanding and could this work against the child's best interests? Did they select an appropriate school for the child and will they get the school of their choice? It is often at this stage that parents seek the support of a partnership worker.

Many LEAs have appointed parent-partnership workers whose role is to ease the parents' journey through the whole process. Sometimes they are employed on a voluntary basis and are usually required to be good communicators with strong listening skills and a working knowledge of the statutory assessment procedures. They can work with parents and advise them of their rights, help them with report writing and attend meetings with them as a support.

Nowadays, parents are becoming much more empowered and aware of the rights of their child to access mainstream education. Authorities are trying their best to accommodate this and the government openly supports and encourages inclusive education. Yet in some areas it remains difficult to get appropriate funding to enable such inclusion to work.

In 1997 the Department for Education and Employment (DfEE) issued a green paper, *Excellence for All Children: meeting special educational needs*. This consultation document was designed to collect together the views of all those involved in the education of these special children and the process of the five-stage model. Following an extensive consultation process throughout the country, the Secretary of State produced *Meeting Special Educational Needs: a programme of action* (1998) stating that a revised code of practice was to come into effect during the academic year 1999/2000.

The thrust of the government's policy is to promote the inclusion of children with special educational needs in mainstream schools whenever possible, whilst acknowledging the need for special schools for some children. The emphasis is on more collaboration between mainstream and special schools with the latter being centres of excellence offering outreach support. The DfEE also proposes to revise the five-stage model and to cease to use the term 'stage' as can be taken to imply that progress for a child equates to moving up the stages. It is the government's aim to reduce the proportion of children requiring statements and, instead, for their special educational needs to be met by resources diverted to mainstream schools for this purpose.

We now have a legislative and philosophical climate that supports inclusive education. Yet, understandably, Head teachers, their staff and the parents of children who are disabled and non-disabled continue to have reservations.

Will adequate resources be made available in mainstream schools? Will the education of children without disabilities suffer as a result? Will it be more work for class teachers? Will the child with disability be disadvantaged by not attending a 'special school' where resources and expertise are readily available to them? Will children who do attend a special school be marginalised together with their families?

We hope that by telling Hannah's story we can allay some of these fears and, through this book, show how, with the right level and type of support, a child with severe learning disability and substantial physical impairment can be educated successfully in a mainstream infant school.

3 Hannah's story

It is now time to introduce you to Hannah and her family. We learnt this story from many discussions with her mother who generously shared with us the experience of having a child with Down's syndrome. In order to write this book we felt we needed some background to Hannah's birth and early years. Her mother, Mrs Levy, talked to us freely and openly about the feelings and experiences she and her husband had. We outline the story here to give you a picture of Hannah and the remarkable family in which she is growing up.

Hannah Ruth was born on 4th August 1989. She weighed 6lbs 4oz.

She arrived in the early hours of the morning after a long labour. The hospital had become concerned about the baby's heartbeat and had moved the delivery on. As soon as Hannah was born, she was rushed away for various tests. When she was brought back, her

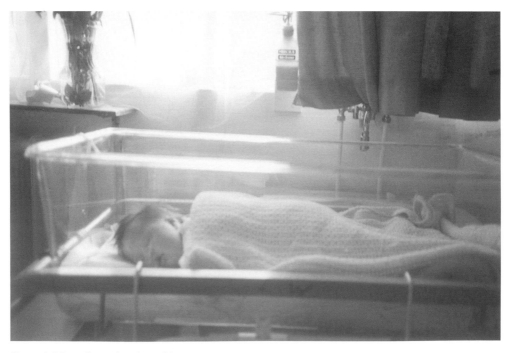

Figure 1 Hannah – a few days old

mother noticed her features. Mrs Levy had been working, on a voluntary basis, with adults with learning difficulties including Down's syndrome, so these features were quite familiar to her. She asked the midwife: 'If she has Down's syndrome will you tell us now?' The Levys were told that there were concerns about some of Hannah's features and the consultant would see her in the morning. That was at 5.00 a.m. From then until 9.00 a.m., when the consultant arrived, Mr and Mrs Levy sat and talked while Hannah lay sleeping.

At 9.00 a.m. the consultant told them that she thought that Hannah probably did have Down's syndrome but that blood tests were needed to confirm it. She left them alone to have time together and gave them their own telephone.

The Levys had not phoned any of their family yet to tell them of the birth. They now had to break the news that their new-born baby had Down's syndrome. The blood test consequently confirmed this.

Mr and Mrs Levy were given their own room at the hospital where a stream of visitors arrived throughout the day and evening. They were well supported by family and friends. A dedicated nursery nurse spent a large part of that first weekend helping Mrs Levy to breast feed Hannah. This was difficult because, like other Down's syndrome babies, she had a poor sucking reflex. Mrs Levy however, was determined to try to do it.

When Hannah was ten days old she was referred to a specialist heart unit. A murmur had been detected by the medical staff and needed investigation. Her attendance at the unit was a dreadful experience. Hannah had to undergo a number of procedures, including an echocardiogram, and Mr and Mrs Levy were at a loss; none of the procedures were explained to them and they did not know what to expect. Hannah was expected to lie still and the doctor expressed surprise and irritation that Mrs Levy did not have a dummy to give her. In front of a large number of students the Levys were told that Hannah had a major heart problem and that, although heart surgery could be carried out, it was not recommended for children with Down's syndrome. This was said to be because 'as the child gets older their quality of life is not good and the operation is not worth it'.

The consultant closed by saying they could see the hospital social worker.

Feeling devastated and shocked – this hospital experience was far worse for them than being told Hannah had Down's syndrome – Mr and Mrs Levy went back to the hospital where Hannah was born. A supportive and caring social worker suggested they should get a second opinion. Thus encouraged and emboldened, the family went to a specialist children's hospital where the experience was far more positive. The same tests were performed with the same result, but Mr and Mrs Levy were treated very differently: there was no discrimination. Hannah was a child first, Down's syndrome came second. And this time her parents were included in all of the processes and discussions.

Mr and Mrs Levy were faced with the first of the many agonising decisions they have had to make throughout Hannah's life. Without heart surgery, the pressure on Hannah's lungs would become intolerable and she would probably not live beyond her teens. With this news, the decision was made for them. She would have the surgery. It could not be performed until Hannah weighed at least 10 lbs and she was putting on weight very slowly, often only taking 1 oz of milk at a time from the bottle. To prevent further damage to her lungs she underwent a minor procedure on one of her main blood vessels while she was under 10 lbs. During this surgery an extra blood vessel was found. This is unusual and is found in only a very small number of cases but it was dealt with successfully. Hannah spent some time in intensive care following this surgery. But she made a full recovery. She was six months old.

Figure 2 Hannah's first birthday party

At 14 months, Hannah weighed enough to have her major heart surgery. She had generally been a robust and healthy baby.

When she went in for the operation she was fit and the surgery went well. However, there were post-operative complications. In Intensive Care, she suffered a cardiac arrest – a most terrifying and frightening experience for her parents who were present at the time. She was successfully resuscitated. Hannah then developed flu-like symptoms and an infection from an intravenous line in her neck. She was seriously ill and became very floppy. Mrs Levy recalls that Hannah was constantly being prodded and poked, having blood taken from her and monitoring equipment attached. It is little wonder that Hannah now has a great fear and dislike of people in white coats.

Hannah has never fully recovered from this episode. Prior to her surgery she had good muscle tone and was a strong baby. She could lift her head and was constantly making babbling noises and developing her language skills like any 14 month old. Now she was floppy when her mother took her in her arms; she had stopped her spontaneous babbling noises and was silent most of the time. No one could explain what had caused the deterioration in her gross motor functioning and in her speech.

Over the next few years Hannah regained some of the ground she had lost, as she slowly recovered from her surgery. She eventually built up more muscle tone and by the age of three had learnt to sit up and crawl. She could vocalise some sounds but was never able to develop any control over them and was unable to form any recognisable words.

Since her birth, Hannah's family had worked hard at promoting and encouraging her physical, social and language development. A Portage worker (see Chapter 1) had come in to see Hannah when she was two weeks old and continued until she was five years old. She was positive that even from a very young age a lot can be done to help a child's development. She visited every week giving input into areas such as socialisation, fine and gross motor skills and cognitive skills. In the meantime, Hannah's mother found that there was a Portage training course locally. When Hannah was seven weeks old, Mrs Levy went on a course, with Hannah in tow, and qualified as a Portage worker. Through this course she became even more aware of Hannah's development potential and learnt to set small goals so that Hannah always succeeded.

When Hannah was three years old, her parents started to search for a playgroup or nursery that would be prepared to take her. She was a small child, unable to walk unaided or speak, with hearing aids and thick glasses. A private nursery school was keen to take Hannah, provided she had the support she needed, as she could not manage physically on her own. Volunteers from the community were found to be with Hannah at the nursery a couple of times a week. Because this was a voluntary service it could not always be relied upon and Mrs Levy would sometimes have to go. This was quite difficult to organise, as when Hannah was nearly two, Ari, the first of four brothers, was born. Ari's arrival did not seem to have any negative effect on Hannah. He soon caught up with her in size and the Levys were often asked if they were twins; fairly soon, Ari overtook his sister in size and development. The Levys knew this would happen but at the same time it was difficult to accept.

The Local Educational Authority agreed to allow Hannah to delay starting school. She could remain at the nursery for a further year until she was six. The Authority also agreed to give funding for Hannah to have support. For a year, between Hannah's fifth and sixth birthday, a friend of Mrs Levy, who was a Portage worker and knew Hannah, worked as her support. It was an ideal solution.

Hannah's time at the nursery was very happy. The children accepted her – the only question they asked was why she wore nappies. Hannah was invited to parties and her mother went with her. The first party invitation was of immense significance to the Levys. This apparently minor event marked the beginning of Hannah's social life.

Hannah was five when Noah, her second brother, was born, and she loved cuddling him and helping to change his nappy. With two brothers to contend with (and two more who were born later) Mr and Mrs Levy were keen for Hannah to retain her 'girlyness'. She enjoyed playing with her brothers' cars but her parents ensured she had a pink bedroom, filled with cuddly toys and dolls, where she could retreat with her girlfriends.

So Hannah had completed her baby and toddler stages. She was now a smiling, cheerful, six year old and was ready to embark on the life of a schoolgirl. One thing was very clear: Hannah's parents did not want her to go to a special school, and finding the right school was not going to be easy.

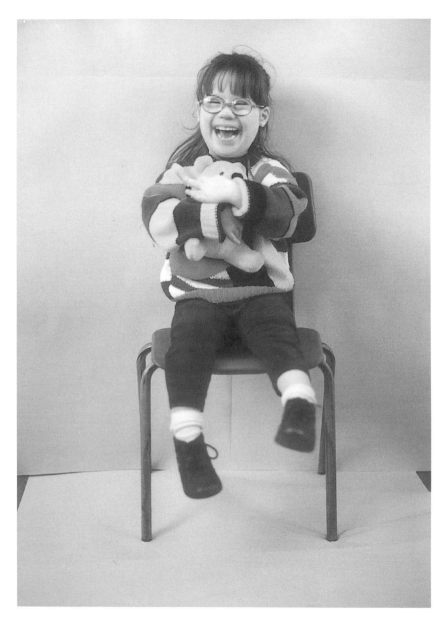

Figure 3 Hannah – nearly a schoolgirl

4 Finding a school

Finding the right school for any child causes days and nights of anxiety to most parents. It is one of the most important decisions they have to make. When a child has disabilities and is going to require a high level of support, finding the right school can be even more difficult.

This decision was particularly hard in Hannah's case because many people, including the professionals who worked with her, felt that there was no chance of her getting into a mainstream school. Hannah's first statement at the age of five recommended the local special school for children with severe learning difficulties. Hannah's parents did not want her to go to a special school.

So, where was Hannah going to go after a happy and successful time at nursery?

The natural choice was the mainstream school attached to the nursery where most of Hannah's friends were going. It was here that Hannah's parents experienced the first of many negative responses. As they were shown around the school all the problems were pointed out. The doors were not wide enough to accommodate Hannah's walking frame; there were too many steps; the physical environment was not suitable. Her parents realised that the school was not willing to take her on.

The Levy's local primary, Trafalgar Infant School, was also approached. It seemed likely that this school would also feel that it could not cater for her physical disabilities. It was decided at the same time to look for a school on religious grounds. At first the story from the religious schools was the same. There was no way Hannah's needs could be met.

Then, at last, a school was found. It was a religious mainstream school whose ethos was to integrate children with special needs. It involved a long journey back and forth each day but otherwise it sounded perfect. The school was concerned, however, about the level of support Hannah would be given. The Levy's Local Education Authority (LEA) agreed to fund one-to-one full-time support. This amount of support for one child was unprecedented and even took Hannah's parents by surprise. The statement was written, and arrangements were made. Hannah was offered a place in the school, along with her brother, Ari. They were to start at the same time. Her parents were greatly relieved that the search was over. School uniforms were bought and final arrangements made. Ten days before brother and sister were due to start, the offer of a place for Hannah was withdrawn. When faced with the reality, the school felt unable to accommodate Hannah after all.

Her parents were devastated. Their children were about to start school, and suddenly they had nowhere to go. Through last minute negotiations, Ari was offered a place at Trafalgar Infant School and was able to start there immediately. Hannah's parents decided to home-educate her while they tried to find a way through the situation.

They sought advice. What the school had done was illegal. There followed months of letters and document exchanges in preparation for a court case. Just before the hearing, Hannah's place at the school was re-instated. The Levys had won their battle. But the trust between school and parents had been irreparably damaged. Hannah's parents did not want her to go there after the way the school had behaved. They declined the offer.

In their original search for schools, the Levys had approached Trafalgar Infant School for Hannah, and had not been declined. They decided to explore the possibility of a place there for Hannah.

Lynne Thompson, the Head teacher at Trafalgar Infant School, presents the school's perspective:

> My first recollection of Hannah is watching her crawl across the floor, in between activities, in her nursery school. I was there, with the Special Needs Co-ordinator (SENCO) at the request of Hannah's mother. The idea was for us to see Hannah in a school-type environment in order to inform our decision about Hannah starting at Trafalgar.
>
> Prior to my visit to the nursery, Mrs Levy had made an appointment to see me. She explained about Hannah's difficulties, but said that she was extremely keen for Hannah to attend Trafalgar Infant School. She said she knew that the school had a very good reputation locally and had a particular ethos that she felt would suit Hannah's needs. Although I could understand Mrs Levy's desire to see Hannah at Trafalgar, I stressed that, as a school managed by the Local Education Authority, any decisions would have to be taken in complete partnership with that Authority. Mrs Levy agreed but could foresee problems convincing them about the suitability of a placement for Hannah at a mainstream school. Mrs Levy left saying that she would be talking with the LEA, but, because of Hannah's special needs, they were also thinking about the possibility of a religious school, some distance away, which catered for such children.
>
> Mrs Levy returned some months later. She reported that arrangements with the religious school had been progressing in conjunction with the LEA; however there had been some problems. They no longer felt comfortable sending Hannah there, despite having a place.
>
> Negotiations for Hannah to attend Trafalgar now began with the LEA. I felt very much caught in the middle between the family and the Authority. I had to be very clear about the level of support Hannah would need if she were to come to Trafalgar. From that first view of Hannah in her nursery, I knew a little of what the school would be taking on.
>
> It was a difficult situation. The family needed to feel supported, I needed to make sure the LEA felt the school was supporting their point of view, and I had to keep in mind, first and foremost, the effect the placement would have on the whole school. Fortunately, the Levy family was aware of these tensions and worked hard with the LEA. In return the LEA appreciated their attitude. It was decided that Hannah could attend Trafalgar.
>
> We then had to spend a lot of time hammering out the smallest detail with regard to her level of support. This proved time consuming as it was a precedent and there was no one to call on who had done it all before. We worked out, in terms of hours and minutes, what 'full-time support' would mean. Hannah was also assigned teaching support as well as classroom assistant support. Practical modifications would be needed to the building and equipment.

Hannah's parents and the LEA also agreed, on our request, that Hannah should have a phased transition into the school. She would start in the summer term in Reception on a part-time basis and gradually work up to full-time in September when she moved to Year 1. We felt this was important for the school. Also from a practical point of view it gave us time to advertise and recruit suitable members of staff.

It was now time to inform all the staff of what would be happening. There was a very mixed reaction. A couple of teachers were very supportive, a couple of others very sceptical. The majority thought it would be OK, as long as she was not in their class until they felt more confident and knew more about Hannah.

The process of advertising for and selecting the staff was daunting. The SENCO and I had really no idea what criteria should be included. The head of the original school suggested for Hannah [for children with severe learning difficulties] was generous with his time. He helped us firstly with advertising, then with short listing and finally with interviewing.

Due to practical issues such as covering lunch breaks it became apparent that full-time classroom assistant support meant that we would require a job share. We were fortunate enough to recruit two staff with different but complimentary skills.

The specialist teaching post was another challenge. We were not sure how the post would work and had to 'create' the job specification with the teacher once they had started. The class chosen for Hannah for Year 1 needed careful thought. The class teacher(s) would have to have a very positive attitude, be flexible, creative and capable of working closely with a large number of different people. These included the school SENCO, two classroom assistants, a special needs teacher and a host of outside agencies that would be visiting the classroom. Finally the choice of actual classroom had to be carefully thought about because of physical aspects such as size and access to toilets and the outside.

The process of Hannah attending Trafalgar Infant School took many months and involved numerous meetings and hours of preparation, all taking place against a background of 'stepping into the unknown'. It started with that initial interview with Mrs Levy. It ended with Hannah starting full-time in her Year 1 class. She had her full compliment of support staff and a curriculum mapped out to meet her needs.

It is a great tribute to all the personnel involved that Hannah's time in the school was such an unqualified success both for Hannah and the whole school community.

Lynne Thompson
Head teacher, Trafalgar Infant School

So Hannah's parents had done it. They had fought for what they believed to be the right education for Hannah. Against all the odds they had secured a place in mainstream education for their daughter who not only had Down's syndrome but also severe mobility and communication difficulties. Their child had been granted full-time support and additional specialist teacher input.

Now they could stop and take a breath and let Hannah show everyone that she could make a success of it.

5   Hannah arrives

The decision had been made: Hannah was due to start her mainstream education at Trafalgar Infant School in the second half of the summer term 1996. She was nearly seven years old. But there were no resources in place and the school had not had time to make preparations. As a parent-helper and an ex-nurse I was approached. Would I be willing to take on the short-term contract as Hannah's classroom support for the last weeks of the summer term? It would allow her to be in school while the recruitment process was carried out and procedures set in place.

I accepted the position. After all, it was only going to be for a couple of months, or so I thought at the time. As Hannah could not speak, her means of communication were non-verbal, and included signing from the Makaton Language Development Project (see Chapter 7). I was given two one-hour training sessions on this signing by the senior speech and language therapist in the area. I was now ready to meet Hannah.

She was placed in Silver Room, a reception class, and paid a short visit the week before the half-term break. This enabled her to meet everyone and experience story time at the end of the day. Her mother left her with her new class for the last 20 minutes of the day and collected her with all the other parents.

I was waiting in the classroom, having been briefly introduced to the other children the afternoon before. I knew the school as my own daughter had been a pupil there a couple of years previously, and I had often helped with reading. But this was different. I was employed now and how would I manage with a little girl who couldn't speak or even walk on her own? I was a nurse but I was not experienced in dealing with children with special needs. This was a new challenge.

I was sitting on one of those tiny infant seats, the children were sitting on the carpet and the class teacher was just about to read a story. Hannah's mother appeared at the glass door and walked in holding Hannah by the hand. My first impression of Hannah was how small she was and how her thick glasses seemed to dominate her little face. She was shy and looked down the whole time as her mother led her to a space on the carpet. The teacher welcomed them and introduced them to the class and me; then her mother left. The teacher explained what we were doing and got the storybook out. I moved my chair so that I was nearby Hannah and watched her as the story was told. She kept her head down throughout. She also made some rather loud noises with her breathing at times, which rather alarmed all of us. At one stage Hannah pulled her glasses off and seemed to have great trouble getting them back on. Do I do it for her? Do I let her struggle? This was to be the first of many decisions regarding the dilemma of promoting Hannah's independence without having expectations that were beyond her capabilities.

Hannah was only to spend the mornings, from 8.55 to 12.00, in school each day for that half of the summer term. Her classmates stayed for the whole school day but this was felt to be too much for Hannah at first. As her mother had educated her at home she had never been to school before. She arrived on Monday looking very smart in her green and grey school uniform. Her mother kissed her at the classroom door, Hannah willingly took my hand and we walked into Silver Room.

Figure 4 Hannah's glasses

She had her own green folder for her reading book and we found out from the class teacher which box she should keep it in. Hannah needed help to lift it up into the box. It was to be several days before she could control her hand enough to do this small movement unaided.

We kept her home-school diary in her reading folder too. This was a small communications book that was filled in at home and at a school. It was written from Hannah's point of view. Her mother might write, 'I went swimming at the weekend and my cousins came to tea'. We could then relay to Hannah's parents how her day at school had gone: 'I enjoyed singing today and I worked hard on my letters'.

As well as having glasses, Hannah had two hearing aids and leg supports which were worn over her socks and strengthened the lower half of both legs. Her shoes fitted on top of them. Her mother gave us three pages of information regarding Hannah's needs. These were invaluable; they gave us the basics so that we knew a little of what to expect. Hannah's mother also taught me two essential signs that she used a lot at home: toilet and drink. She explained how Hannah would ask to go to the toilet and what help she needed. Hannah was not having milk at school, as cow's milk seemed to make her produce more mucous in her nasal passages. Instead she was to have water from a beaker which she managed with a little support and a lot of tissues.

We were asked to encourage Hannah to walk and not to let her crawl around the classroom. In order to walk she needed to hold on to furniture or someone's hand or to use her frame. This was brought in on that first day and remained with Hannah at school. She had a duplicate one at home and this saved having to transport her frame back and forth each day. The frame was made of stainless steel with a wheel on each of its four corners. Hannah held it in front of her and pushed it to move forward. It was referred to as her 'zimmie'. It was rather cumbersome for the classroom but was invaluable in the vast playground.

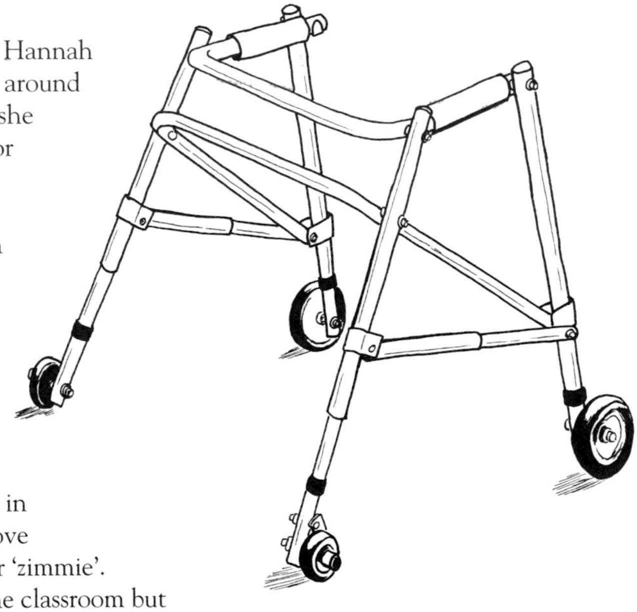

Figure 5 Hannah's first walking frame

Hannah remained rather shy for these first few days and initially would try and climb up onto my lap. Eventually I decided to sit next to her on the carpet with the other children or on a small chair beside her at the table. She seemed to need the physical comfort of having me on her level and this gave her confidence. We spent a lot of time in the toilet and at the water fountain before I realised that this was a ploy of Hannah's and nothing to do with her bladder control. The most useful sign I discovered from Hannah's mother during those first days was 'later'!

Slowly Hannah became more at ease with the other children and no longer sat with her head bowed. She looked around and took an interest in what was going on. The children realised that they could talk to her and be understood and I shared my small knowledge of Makaton signs with them. I soon realised that Hannah had a very good understanding of what was being said to her, even without the signing. The purpose of the signing was for her to learn signs to communicate back to us.

During that first week I was invited by Hannah's mother to visit them at home. The teacher for children with hearing impairment was coming to do a session with Hannah and her mother thought I might find it useful to observe them working together. I found it extremely useful to see Hannah in her own environment and observe the way her mother and the teacher used signs with her. She was going over the concepts of 'inside' and 'outside'. Hannah would not work when her mother was in the room but was able to focus when she left. I also realised what discomfort Hannah had to tolerate with her leg supports. As soon as she was home she wanted to relax and take them off.

School assembly was a challenging time for Hannah. It was held in a big hall that could be noisy and her attention wandered quite easily. I went in with her and initially I sat on the floor beside her. Quite often we had to leave as she became too restless and started crawling away. If there was singing she was able to sit through the assembly which lasted about 15 minutes. She loved listening to the children singing and this was to be a very special time later on when the whole school learnt to sign with Hannah as they sang the words of their songs. After a few weeks, towards the end of term, she was more confident and able to sit still, role modelling the other children. I could sit apart from her on a seat as long as I was fairly nearby. Sometimes, however, when she found it a bit long and boring, she would have a 'coughing fit' so that I took her out!

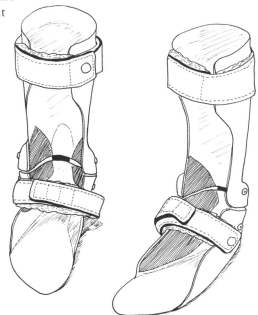

Figure 6 Hannah's leg supports

At play time, Hannah used her frame to get about. She needed help getting out of the door of Silver Room, as there was a step to manoeuvre down. Once on the tarmac, she could choose where to go and get herself there. She usually chose one of the playhouses and at first I went with her. Other children throughout the school were very interested in

Hannah and sometimes there would be a large crowd around her. This caused her to bury her face away and sometimes get upset. Gradually, the children learnt to give her space.

Like any other child, Hannah loved to play. During those first days we made up two games. The 'ice-cream' game involved Hannah holding out her hand as a bowl and me serving her with scoops of ice-cream, pouring chocolate sauce over it and sprinkling nuts on top. She then served me. This was a very popular game and other children tried to play this with Hannah. At first she was reluctant and insisted I played, but gradually she let them 'in' on the game. The other was the doctor game which involved me pretending to be a rather arrogant doctor who spoke down to her while taking her pulse, listening to her chest and taking blood from the back of her hand. She found this surprisingly amusing and often giggled throughout the whole interaction. Hannah had spent many months in hospital undergoing difficult and sometimes quite painful procedures. It was a unique experience to see her able to enjoy a joke related to what must have been a very distressing time for her.

When the bell went for the end of play Hannah stayed in the playhouse and was very reluctant to move. I accepted this at first and used only gentle encouragement to get her out. As I got to know Hannah and her robust sense of self, I realised I could be quite a lot firmer and soon we were walking back to class with everyone else.

In Hannah's third week, she was visited in class by her physiotherapist and occupational therapist. They were delighted to see her but she was unusually unco-operative with them. We thought it was probably because she was experiencing two separate parts of her life together – the medical side and the education side – and she wasn't quite sure how to react. They adjusted the height of the footstool that had been provided for Hannah so that her whole feet, and not just her toes, were supported and her knees were level with her bottom when sitting. This helped her to adopt a much more upright sitting position and appeared more comfortable for her. They also talked to us about Hannah's gross and fine motor skills. She could not yet stand unsupported as she found it difficult to maintain her balance. She also found controlling a pencil very demanding. Later, the physiotherapist gave us a programme to improve Hannah's balance when she was kneeling. Kneeling had to be mastered before she could balance when standing. It was several months before Hannah had a sloping desktop and a wrist support to help her with her handwriting.

The following week the speech therapist visited Hannah at school. She observed her in the classroom and they did some speech work. For the first time I realised just how difficult it was for Hannah to control her mouth. They played a game in which Hannah had to stick out her tongue and lick a piece of sticky paper. She found it almost impossible to open her mouth at the required time and put out her tongue. I could see her concentrating, summoning all her control, but her tongue stayed where it was. It reminded me of a recent trip to my dentist when, with a numb mouth, I was asked to rinse using the mouthwash. My lack of control was a shock to me, I couldn't stop it dribbling! Here was Hannah trying her hardest to lick a piece of paper and appearing to have the same lack of control. Learning to speak was going to be an enormous challenge for her.

The first half-term flew by. Hannah joined in all the activities in Silver Room. She changed for P.E. with all the other children, the only difference being that she kept on her leg supports and did not have plimsoles to wear. She found the physical activity quite tiring and sometimes we had to sit out towards the end. She worked on writing and numeracy skills, although we were really feeling our way to begin with. Should she be attempting cursive writing at all? The other children were. But it seemed too big a task for Hannah. We stuck to the general formation of 'c', 'a', 'n' and 'h'. Hannah loved the computer and we spent a lot of her time playing counting games and getting her used to what the keys did. She was a very fast learner and could concentrate for long periods of time. Sometimes Hannah had a session in the home corner if she finished her work. She would immediately pick up the dolly and play mother and baby games. It was in the home corner that Hannah was first seen to maintain interaction with other children for any length of time.

After four or five weeks, Hannah had learnt when it was play time and when she had to get down to work. She was becoming more independent on the computer and was working on different ways of getting out of assembly! During week six, her special needs teacher visited. She was to work with Hannah for half of each school day, starting in the autumn term. Her first comment was that Hannah had to be weaned off me. And I had tried so hard! But I knew she was right. What Hannah needed was support that was in the background, giving her the chance to be as independent as possible and to make relationships with her peers. She would do that much more easily if I backed off a little. That remained the challenge. For Hannah to be safe and able to access the whole curriculum, with support only when it was absolutely necessary.

Key points

- Gradually build up child's time in school.
- Information from parents is invaluable in giving a picture of the child, their likes and dislikes, strengths and weaknesses.
- Spend time each day talking with the child's carer, raising any issues of concern.
- 'Listen' to the child's non-verbal communication. They will show you when there is a problem.
- Do not worry at first if the child is not producing very much work. The important thing for them is that they become accustomed to the routine of the school day.
- Build up trust between you by 'being there' for the child. Respond quickly when they are upset and do not be afraid to cuddle them if they seem to want this.
- Ensure that the child realises that you are there to help them when they cannot do it by themselves but you are not a personal servant!
- Be honest and straightforward with the child and tell them when you have a problem, e.g. 'I don't think you need the toilet again Hannah. I think you are just fed up with writing'.
- Keep a notebook and write a few lines summarising the notable events of those first few weeks in school.
- Set up a communication book between home and school and write in it as if you are the child – do this with the active involvement of the child. 'I managed to sit through the whole of assembly today. I really enjoyed the singing.'
- Use humour liberally and encourage lots of laughter.

6 The school responds

During Hannah's easing-in period, the school had the task of ensuring that personnel and systems were put in place for a smooth inclusion. There were meetings between Lynne Thompson, Trafalgar's Head teacher, Mr and Mrs Levy, the Special Educational Needs Co-ordinator (SENCO), the Head of the school for 'severe learning difficulties' (SLD) originally recommended for Hannah, and the head of a local special school who was acting as an LEA inspector. Mrs Levy's expectations for Hannah were discussed, alongside how the school was going to structure the high level of support she was to receive. A specialist teacher and full-time classroom support had to be found. Advice was given by the Head of the special school on the wording of recruitment advertisements to be placed in a local newspaper (classroom support job advertisement – Appendix 1). Job descriptions were drawn up for these positions (classroom support job description – Appendix 2) and the staff were to start in the autumn term.

The advertisement for the Special Educational Needs classroom support received a huge response. After careful selection and consideration by the interview panel (Head teacher, SENCO, school governor and Head of the local SLD school), it was decided that the job should be shared between two people. I was already in the school working, part-time with a different child with special needs and had seen Hannah with her temporary classroom support. We both applied for the position and were thrilled to be appointed to share the job.

The interview for Hannah's specialist teacher took place at the end of that summer term. A woman with experience of teaching in special schools was appointed. She was aware that bringing the skills from a special school into mainstream education was unknown territory and we would all, therefore, be pooling our resources to make this work.

The conversion of the classroom support role into a job share was one of the most important decisions to have been taken at this early stage. Once we were in place as Hannah's SEN classroom support we soon discovered that the job, whilst rewarding and stimulating, could be very demanding, both physically and emotionally. It would have been virtually impossible for one person to carry out alone. Two of us working closely together, albeit at different times of the day, were able to share our joint experiences, discuss important issues and develop our approach to make our input into Hannah's school life most productive. We were able to share the difficulties and celebrate the successes together. This teamwork allowed the SENCO and class teachers to work as closely as possible to their normal routines with minimum disruption to the school as a whole.

There are some essential qualities required in candidates being considered for SEN classroom support, and the interview panel looked for these. Both of us had had some level of experience with children with special needs, but it is important to note how the following personal qualities were more important than any qualifications or experience we may have had:

*   enthusiasm – needed in abundance – through good times and bad
*   patience – this is not a quick process. Sometimes things do not appear to be changing despite your very best efforts
*   positive approach and determination – children are quick to spot any lack of these in any member of school staff. For the SEN support, it is even more important to promote motivation
*   sense of humour – terribly important – the job can be very difficult at times, and it is essential to be able to keep smiling throughout
*   sensitivity – there are often issues to be raised with the child or their parents and it is important to be sensitive to their concerns
*   flexibility – essential when working in a team
*   calmness – panicking helps no one when things aren't going right or there's a problem.

We found that it was important for both of us in the job share to be able to work together and develop a trusting relationship. If we were concerned or excited about something that had happened during the day that there had been no chance to discuss, we talked about it on the telephone in the evening. Our close co-ordination was not only good from the point of view of our work effort, but also helped greatly with our relationship with Hannah. She, after all, was going to have to deal with both of us. Through this approach, we were able to ensure consistency and good communication. This helped gain Hannah's trust and set up a close bond with her.

It was during this time that the detailed planning and organisation for Hannah's inclusion took place. The school's commitment to making the situation work was strong and determined but, equally, the school was very apprehensive of the task that lay ahead. The responsibility to Hannah, the other children in the school, their parents and the staff was immense. The school was breaking new ground.

The school staff had very real concerns and needed details on how the inclusion was to work and how it would affect them in their everyday activities. The SENCO and Head teacher played an important role in identifying where the staff's concerns lay, and putting in procedures to allay them.

To find out just what school staff and governors thought at this early stage, we have carried out a survey as part of our research for this book. We wanted to find out how their reactions changed from the time before Hannah arrived at the school to how they were just after she had left two years later.

The survey revealed that 80 per cent of the staff and governors had questions and real concerns before Hannah started at school. The main issues were:

*   Would the school be able to meet Hannah's special needs?
*   How would we address the general lack of experience of working with children with special needs?
*   How much extra work would Hannah create, particularly for the class teacher?
*   How would time be divided between Hannah and other class members?

- What would be the reaction of other children to Hannah?
- How would Hannah's progress be monitored?
- General fear of the unknown.

By the time Hannah had left the school, these feelings had changed dramatically. Without exception, staff and governors alike felt that this had been a successful and fulfilling experience. A summary of the results are shown at the end of this chapter.

But allaying the fears of the staff was just one problem area to overcome. Once Hannah started school there was a vast range of organisational issues that needed to be addressed. These could have become quite overwhelming had it not been for the high level of specialist teaching and SEN classroom support that Hannah received. This enabled the SENCO to spend time in the overall management of the project and the class teachers to treat Hannah as part of the whole class.

It was the SENCO who was responsible for co-ordinating contacts with the educational psychologist, speech and language therapist, occupational therapist, physiotherapist, Head teacher, class teachers, specialist teacher, SEN classroom support and parents, and to organise the IEP reviews. She also organised the alterations that were necessary to allow Hannah to move around the school, such as the handrails and ramps recommended by the occupational therapist and then assessed by the Health and Safety Department. As the school is a one-storey building the structural changes and amount of special equipment required for Hannah were minimal.

Hannah's family provided the SENCO with a complete list of contact details of those individuals and organisations who had provided assistance for Hannah in the past. Several of these had made home visits to Hannah regularly since she was very small, and they had become familiar, friendly faces to her.

It was reassuring for us to meet people who had known Hannah since she was a baby. They could fill gaps in our knowledge and help us build a complete picture of Hannah. Appointments were made for them to assess Hannah in her new setting. It was important that these meetings were timed carefully so that too many visitors did not disrupt the class in one day.

Accurate and relevant recording procedures are a very important aspect of the day-to-day management of any special needs child. These allow proper assessment of a child's work and progress and form the basis for on-going and formal reviews. However, in Hannah's case, it was essential to set up procedures that allowed the monitoring of the work to be seamless. There were many people involved, and many were on a job share or part-time basis. For example, her class teachers for Year 1 and 2 and the SEN classroom supports were job sharing, and the SENCO and specialist teacher were part-time. Anyone starting their 'shift' would be required to know exactly what the current situation was, as well as being fully aware of the overall targets and aims that the school had established for Hannah.

At the beginning of Year 1, a simple diary system was installed which was a continuation of the approach that had been successfully piloted when Hannah had attended Reception. This diary was completed by the SEN classroom support at the end of each morning or afternoon and recorded briefly what Hannah had done during the day, how focused she had been, her interaction skills and her general mood. Because the diary was always up-to-date and readily available to all, it provided a simple and effective way of keeping all parties fully informed of Hannah's progress with relatively little fuss or effort. Inevitably there were times when someone had not, or could not, update their section for various reasons, and as time went on there were some fairly irrelevant and obscure entries such as, 'Hannah had two coughing fits today', or 'Not such a good day today'. However, as we reviewed the system during the first few weeks, entries became more appropriate.

As Hannah started to develop her skills and work more closely to the National Curriculum framework, it became clear that a structured recording system was needed. By the middle of the first term of Year 1, Hannah's specialist teacher had prepared her Individual Educational Plan (IEP) (Appendix 3). Based on this, a separate recording sheet for each IEP was completed (Appendix 4). We also had a separate daily record sheet for any unusual occurrences. The daily record sheet was set up to show more of the qualitative aspects of Hannah's work – how she was feeling generally and her patterns of behaviour. This proved to be an informative document, reminding us of some of the most important aspects of Hannah's behaviour; for example that, by Friday, she was often feeling very tired (Appendix 5).

Within a matter of days we could see the benefits of this new approach to record keeping. The sheets were easy to access, and instantly showed anyone who worked with Hannah how she was feeling, how she was coping with the different areas of her curriculum, where she was working well and where she needed further encouragement with her IEP.

Staff communication was another of the key factors in ensuring Hannah's inclusion ran smoothly and efficiently. In Year 1, our week started at 8.30 a.m. on a Monday when we had a meeting with Hannah's specialist teacher. We kept a minute book for these meetings which was invaluable, especially when it came to seeing who had said they would do what! We also minuted any important conversations we had had, particularly with Hannah's mother. We planned and monitored Hannah's work for that week. Using Hannah's IEP record book we looked at what Hannah had done, what she had found easy, and what she had found challenging. We then decided what work should be reinforced. We discussed any meetings with outside agencies that had taken place and how we would implement any required changes. These meetings continued in Year 2 with the SENCO after the specialist teacher had left.

Planning happened once a week when all the year group teachers would meet to discuss and organise the following week's work. One of us would attend these meetings where we learnt what the children would be taught and discussed how work could be differentiated to make it suitable for Hannah.

As both classroom support assistants were in school on a Monday morning, one of us had an hour to prepare resources for the lessons that week. This involved finding books and enlarging work sheets relevant to the topic being covered. This was also a good time for liaison with Hannah's mother. The other classroom assistant would go to meet Hannah in her class at 8.55 a.m.

Years 1 and 2 presented two very different situations. During the first year we had the specialist teacher in the class for half the week (all day on Mondays, and on Tuesday, Wednesday and Thursday mornings), and benefited from a high level of support. There were many procedures to implement and a vast amount to learn. But Hannah's specialist teacher left for a new job at the end of Year 1 and a replacement could not be found. We, the SEN classroom supports, and the class teachers, had become much more confident in the management of Hannah's day-to-day learning. We decided that we could manage during the second year if the specialist teacher could act as a consultant and come in once a term to observe Hannah and set her new IEPs. This was what we did and even

Hannah's parents agreed that the level of support Hannah was now receiving was more realistic.

It was important to establish from the beginning who we, as SEN classroom supports, should report to. Was it the class teachers, the SENCO or the specialist teacher? For day-to-day learning we liased with the specialist teacher and the class teachers, but when problems arose we sought the help of the SENCO. We worked very much as a team with a flexible 'give and take' framework. The most important aspect was that one of her SEN classroom supports was always with Hannah, ensuring that she was safe and that classroom management was not affected.

As there were so many aspects to Hannah's curriculum, we had different areas of responsibility. One of us was responsible for Hannah's physiotherapy programme and the other for Hannah's speechwork. This smoothed the workload and gave continuity to the programmes and the relationships with different therapists. It also gave us the ability to become fully competent in different areas of Hannah's curriculum. This was particularly beneficial when it came to preparing reports for Hannah's annual review. Those involved with Hannah in school, her parents and outside agencies came together for the review to discuss her progress and formulate plans to meet her future needs. We submitted a report for this meeting (Appendix 6) which was circulated along with others written by her teachers and therapists.

This high level of organisation and the detailed recording systems contributed to the smooth running of Hannah's inclusion. Everyone who had had concerns at the beginning had changed their views by the time Hannah left – a remarkable turnabout. This takes us back to our survey results. The reasons respondents gave for changing their views were as follows:

* A dedicated and organised support team.
* Commitment from the whole staff group.
* Children's interest and care for Hannah; the experience became two-way with advantages for everyone.
* The acceptance of Hannah by other children which helped make her happy and secure.
* Hannah taught the school as much as she learnt.

We had stepped into the unknown, but with a high level of support that enabled us to include a child with such profound difficulties into the life of the school. The attitude of Hannah and her parents contributed greatly to the relative ease with which we worked through the problems that arose. It didn't seem so hard after all.

Key Points

* Be sensitive to staff concerns.
* The task of supporting a child with severe physical and learning difficulty throughout the school day is emotionally and physically demanding. A job share eases the workload.
* Classroom supports should show enthusiasm, patience, a positive approach, determination, sense of humour, sensitivity, flexibility and calmness when working with a child with special needs.
* Get to know and understand the people with whom you are working closely.

- Ensure that accurate and relevant recording procedures are kept up-to-date on a daily basis.
- Refer to the IEP weekly to ensure work is still on target.
- Talk to the different therapists involved and take advantage of their expertise.

7   Talking without speech

Communication is one of the most important aspects of our life. It is easy to take it for granted. We learn to develop our language skills slowly; a tentative attempt at a single word becomes a two-word phrase which is then added to in order to build a sentence. These sentences are often non-grammatical and yet we make ourselves understood. We can ask for a drink, express our dislikes or say something is too difficult and we don't want to carry on. Without communication there are frustrations, difficulties and sometimes disasters. An adult's use of vocabulary and expression of concepts is far more sophisticated than a child's. Children's communication may be limited and there may be a greater use of body language and gesture.

These thoughts were uppermost in our minds when we knew Hannah was coming to our school. How was she going to manage in an environment with over 200 children, when she could not talk and could not hear properly without a hearing aid in each ear? How would we know if she wanted to go to the toilet, if she wanted a drink or what it was that was making her happy or sad? How could we communicate with her?

The speech and language therapists came to the rescue. Makaton, a language development programme using speech, signs and symbols was going to be our main means of communicating with Hannah. She had been using Makaton at home and had a good working knowledge of it. The only problem was, we hadn't!

The Makaton Vocabulary is a complete language programme providing basic communication, promoting language development and stimulating speech. There is a Core Vocabulary of over 350 basic language concepts which are presented in developmental stages so that simple and essential concepts are taught first and more complex ones are introduced gradually. It allows for those concepts learnt as individual signs to be linked together to form short phrases and sentences so that language as a communication tool is taught and experienced. The Core Vocabulary is further enhanced by the Resource Vocabulary, much of which complements the National Curriculum. Makaton Signs are matched to all the concepts in the two vocabularies which are used with speech or the written word.

Originally, Makaton was designed to provide communication for adults who were deaf or with severe learning difficulties. It proved to be so successful that its application was then revised and expanded to cover the needs of children and the community. Normal grammatical speech is spoken alongside Makaton signing even if only key words are being signed. Natural facial expressions and body language are used, so communication is kept as 'normal' as possible, the only difference being the signing.

Makaton was a completely new mode of communication for all of us at the school. A Makaton training session was set up for us by the Speech and Language Therapy Department which proved to be invaluable. The Makaton Vocabulary Development Project

(MVDP) advise that it is essential to attend a Makaton Vocabulary Workshop or to have professional training to be able to derive maximum understanding of the scheme. This was certainly the case with us.

The training was provided for staff during an INSET day when we had a whole afternoon set aside for the Makaton session. This was followed by four further sessions for those staff who were most directly involved with Hannah. At the end of this session we all had a sound basic knowledge of the purpose of Makaton signing and were able to communicate amongst ourselves quite competently. We could all sign at least 'Hello', 'Good morning' and 'What are you doing?'. It is important to realise that unless you are using signing frequently it is very easy to forget. For those working with Hannah more closely it was easier to build up a working vocabulary and there was more incentive to update and regularly revise the signs being used.

Some signs are easy to remember because they appear to be straightforward miming actions:

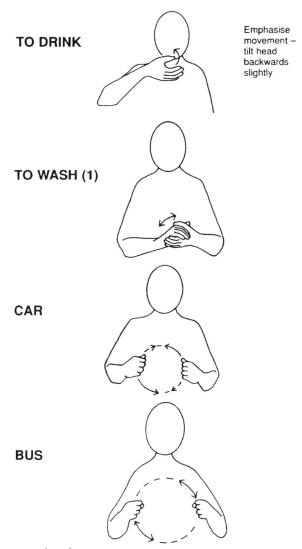

Figure 7   Makaton signs based on mime

Others are more abstract but we were given hints during our Makaton training session on how to remember them.

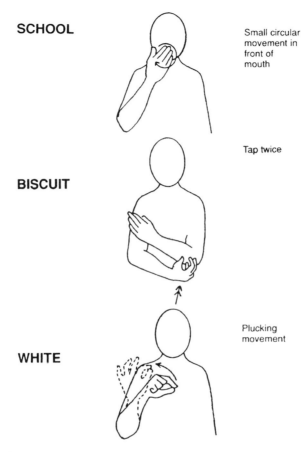

SCHOOL Small circular movement in front of mouth

BISCUIT Tap twice

WHITE Plucking movement

Figure 8   Makaton signs

We were taught the sign for 'biscuit' by miming knocking weevils out of a biscuit and the sign for 'white' by miming plucking a white feather from your jumper.

Other signs simply had to be learnt and remembered.

On my first morning of working with Hannah in Year 1, I nervously greeted her with my tentative signing of 'Hello Hannah, how are you?'

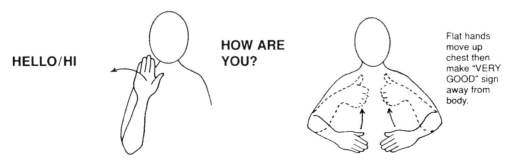

HELLO/HI   **HOW ARE YOU?**   Flat hands move up chest then make "VERY GOOD" sign away from body.

Figure 9   Makaton signs

I signed Hannah's name by finger spelling the letter 'H'. All the children were keen to learn how to sign their own names and we taught them the finger spelling alphabet:

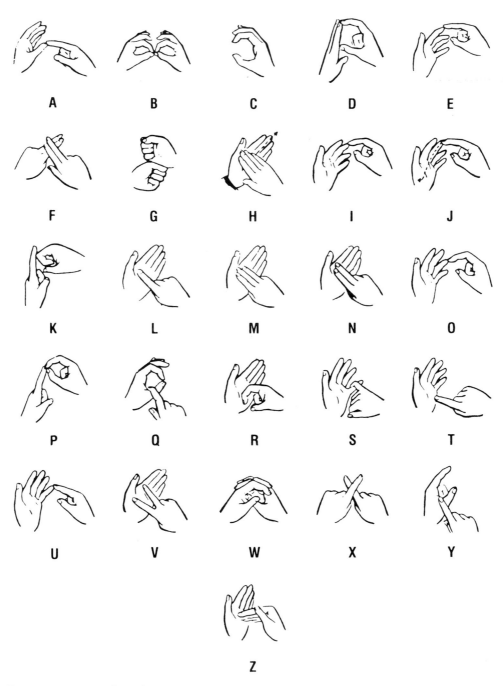

Figure 10   Finger spelling chart

In response to my greeting Hannah smiled and put her thumb up to sign 'OK.'

I can remember feeling tremendous relief that I had made myself understood.

Each morning I would greet her in a similar way as she entered the class, with many of the other children joining in. When the class teacher took the register in the morning and afternoon, she would sign 'Good morning Hannah' and then look for her response. Hannah would sign in reply 'Good morning' followed by the teacher's name. Names were signed by using the initial letter of the person's name by finger spelling.

At the beginning of Year 1, Hannah brought the Makaton Nursery Rhyme Video into school. This features familiar nursery rhymes sung and signed in a clear and lively way. During an afternoon free-activity session, the class of five year olds sat and watched it. Everyone loved it, especially Hannah, as she knew the video well and she could show her classmates how able she was at signing many of the rhymes.

When the class started a new topic, we would spend time learning new and relevant signs from the *Makaton for the National Curriculum* book. When introducing a topic such as electricity or shape, we were able to reinforce information by signing slightly more technical words. When teaching Hannah the new signs, we would teach the whole class – the children were far quicker at grasping signs than many of the school staff! This only took a few minutes but was a valuable skill for them to have and made a more open and comfortable environment for Hannah.

Understanding Hannah's signing at first was particularly difficult because of her poor fine motor skills. However, through Hannah's eagerness and determination to communicate, and in particular her patience, we soon started to understand what she was telling us.

One very beneficial meeting with Hannah's mother was to discuss and co-ordinate signs used at home and school. We had this meeting in the second term of Year 1, but in retrospect it would have been most useful at the beginning of Hannah's school life with us. We were puzzled for the first few weeks when Hannah started covering her eyes with her hands and making very excited noises. This started on a Tuesday and often went through to Friday. We learnt that this was the sign for *Shabbat*, a Jewish celebration which the family observed every Friday and which was the highlight of the week for Hannah. Hannah also had her own sign for the computer, which was different to the Makaton sign. This had evolved from home where she had used a computer frequently and her own sign was familiar to her. There was one particular sign that Hannah used repeatedly, often on a Monday morning. Along with signing she would become very animated and it was only after discussion with her mother that we discovered that this was the sign for Uncle Ardy – a very great favourite of Hannah's. It turned out she was telling us that he had been to her house and they had eaten chocolate ice-cream together!

An important sign we taught Hannah at an early stage was 'I've had enough'. Unlike other children who could say 'I don't want to' or 'Go away', Hannah was unable to express herself verbally. On a couple of occasions she had resorted to biting – much to the distress of her victim, normally a best friend, and to Hannah! On the third biting occasion when we felt our stern words and even those of the class teacher were not reaching Hannah, we took her to see the Head teacher. Perhaps luckily for her, she was not in her office and it fell upon a teacher on the management team to tell her off – and quite severely. It's difficult to know who was most upset – the teacher or Hannah. To have a sign to indicate she had had enough gave Hannah a dignified independence. The new sign was introduced after the telling off and she did not bite again.

The school's philosophy in fully including Hannah gave a platform for all the children to show their eagerness to communicate with her and through their signing allowed the school to develop a positive communicative environment.

Hannah's classmates were particularly able and signed very proficiently. In assembly the whole school would sign 'Good morning Mrs Thompson' and everybody could sign and sing a variety of songs, the most popular being 'Yellow Submarine'. The children were so eager to learn the signs for any new songs that during singing they would turn right round and watch the classroom assistants signing for Hannah and try to copy them.

With her parents and the school's input, Hannah developed a large number of signs and could make known what she wanted and information that she wanted to share. At the beginning of Year 2 we encouraged her to use her signs in a sentence and not just a single sign. We would not accept Hannah signing just 'Toilet', but encouraged and helped her to sign 'I want to go to the Toilet'. Not every single word would be signed but she would use three or four signs to form her sentence:

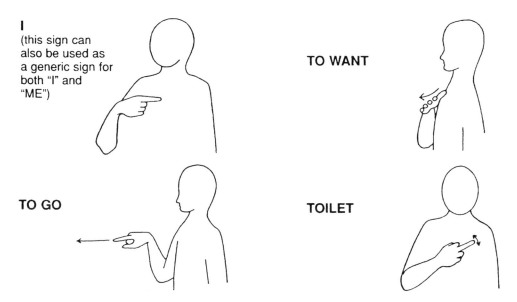

I
(this sign can also be used as a generic sign for both "I" and "ME")

TO WANT

TO GO

TOILET

Figure 7   Makaton signs

As the signing became more complex it was important to give Hannah time to under-stand what had been said and signed to her and to allow her ample time to formulate a reply.

A Makaton pictorial symbol system was introduced to Hannah as an additional means of communication by the speech and language therapist at the end of Year 1. This com-munication system is part of Makaton's multi-modal approach which gave Hannah another means of communicating her needs. It also gave her some variety and choice in her means of communicating and is also a pre-cursor to reading and literacy skills. The symbols were presented with the written word and this aided her sight vocabulary.

It helped develop other skills, such as memory – she had to remember where each symbol was stored in her communications book and also how to access it. It also helped Hannah because of the difficulties she experienced with her fine motor skills. Symbols are easier to manipulate than trying to use signs, and they are permanent and present no ambiguity.

We had three training sessions with the speech and language therapist when we were shown how to use the symbols and to prepare the materials we were to use.

Hannah and I worked on this new form of communication during her speech work session in the form of a shopping game and a lotto game with symbols. We used sets of symbols divided into simple categories – drinking, eating, washing, dressing and playing. In different baskets we included items from each category, such as tea, milk, apple, cake, soap, shampoo, toothpaste, socks, scarf, book and ball. With the relevant symbols laid out in front of her, Hannah would sign that she wanted to buy, for example, a doll. We would exchange the symbol for the doll.

Figure 12   Symbols used by Hannah

(Some of the symbols depicted are Makaton Symbols. Others are not. The MVDP neither encourages nor advocates the mixture of different symbol systems. However, when different systems are used, there is a need to ensure that all users are aware of this, and that there is an agreement on which are chosen and why.)

We also devised a lotto game with a laminated board with six symbols on it and small matching cards which Hannah had to match. These were effective and fun ways to introduce Hannah to this new system.

We later used symbols as a means to help Hannah recall what she had done during her school day and take this information home with her. We used a piece of bright yellow A3 paper which we laminated. Using this landscape, we used two small pieces of velcro centred at the top for the date and two strips widthways for her morning and afternoon activities. We had a large selection of symbols, cut into one inch squares which were also laminated and velcroed; these included the days of the week and months of the year and symbols representing the different activities of Hannah's daily curriculum.

At the end of the afternoon play time, Hannah would prepare her chart by finding the correct date and the order of her school day and sticking down the symbols which we would then reduce and photocopy (Appendix 7). This gave her the opportunity to remember her school day, talk about what she had and hadn't enjoyed, and to share this information when she went home.

This was very much Hannah's own piece of work. It developed her independence as well as increasing and further developing her communication skills.

We did not know, and still do not know, whether Hannah would ever be able to speak; but the language work sessions we followed three times a week were valuable. These occasions when we took Hannah out of the classroom became part of her weekly routine. A child with speech difficulties from a reception class joined us, which Hannah enjoyed. We worked hard and she thoroughly enjoyed doing the mouth and facial exercises which had been set by the speech and language therapist and were reviewed by her every term. These exercises were specifically set for Hannah but could apply to any child who needs to focus on facial and oral awareness to enable the production of accurate, meaningful sounds. We had a varied programme. Here are some examples of a few of Hannah's favourites and in particular those exercises where we could all see results.

- Using a mirror, which was a safety mirror suitable for children, Hannah would practise opening and closing her mouth. To start with I would gently place one hand under her chin and one hand under mine and gently close her, and my, mouth. After a short time she would use her own hand to guide her mouth closed. (Hannah's mother was surprised to find her doing this at home in the evenings in front of a mirror and it was not until we were discussing our speech work programme that all came to light!)
- The next exercise worked on Hannah's fine motor skills as well as her speech work. She would make a small cake out of playdough and then stick a candle in it. I would light the candle for Hannah to blow out. She needed to be supervised very carefully for this as the first time we tried it she very nearly singed her hair. At first she found this virtually impossible, but with practice, and by slowly developing the strength of her blow, the flicker of the candle became greater until she finally blew it out.
- We used different materials on Hannah's face for her to develop facial awareness, which is essential in the development of speech. By using materials such as cotton wool, a make-up brush, a toothbrush and a crinkled piece of paper she learnt to differentiate what was 'rough' and what was 'smooth'.
- Wearing a brightly coloured lipstick, which Hannah loved, she made different shapes with her mouth and then kissed a piece of paper to see the results. During this exercise I discovered I was no make up artist!

- Hannah would cuddle a teddy bear and say 'aaahh'; we encouraged her to keep this sound going for longer by allowing her to cuddle the teddy for the time she was making the sound.

We used these speech sessions to work on Hannah's phonic skills. Even though she found it tremendously difficult to produce speech sounds, she became aware of what sounds were and where they appear in words. This was a fundamental skill in the development of her literacy achievements. We played listening and discrimination games which allowed her to identify sounds in isolation and at the beginning of words. This was another occasion when other children who were struggling with literacy skills joined us and it provided a good opportunity for Hannah to practise turn-taking.

Even though these were formal sessions held three afternoons a week, Hannah was encouraged to vocalise during her normal working day. If she pointed to an object or signed something we would ask her to say it as well.

Having Hannah in school demonstrated how much can be communicated without the ability to speak. By the end of Year 1 she could share a joke with us, show true friendship to her peers, let us know if she was upset or fed-up, happy or excited or she could even just be cheeky. In case we missed the subtle nuances of the latter, she would take her cheek in her thumb and forefinger and give it a pinch. Her way of saying, 'I am being cheeky!'.

Communication with Hannah had been one of our main concerns when she started at the school. We need not have worried. The confidence that evolved from working with the speech and language therapists and Hannah's parents together with Hannah's positive approach, proved our fears to be unfounded.

Key Points

- Continually monitor your vocabulary and gradually add concepts that the child requires.
- Revise signing regularly.
- Co-ordinate the signs used at home with the ones used at school – a meeting with the parents early on is important.
- Introduce a sign for 'I've had enough' early on – something that is simple and easily understood.
- Develop a communicative environment by involving the child's peers in the signing system being used – children love signing and can often pick it up quicker than adults!
- When introducing new signs for a particular topic, take a few minutes to teach the whole class (I used to do this straight after afternoon register).
- When the whole school is singing, make sure the child has a clear view of you and can see you signing.
- Speech sessions should be fun, but can be tiring. Pace the session to the child's level.
- Encourage vocalisation and speech practise during the normal day and not just during speech sessions.
- Encourage the use of multiple signing rather than just single words.

- Don't be afraid to say to a child 'I don't understand – please try again'.
- Do not rush the child – they must know they have time to get over what they want to say.
- Practise if not using signing frequently.

8   Moving around the school

It was important for Hannah to be familiar with the layout of the school. During the first half-term of Year 1 our objective was to ensure that Hannah could find the classes and different areas.

We introduced her 'orientation' programme at the beginning of the afternoon session straight after register. She loved going into the different classes and having a 'chat' with the teachers and children, and quite often it was hard to get her to leave. She learnt all the names of the classes and, after a while, was able to make her own way there with her 'zimmie'. It was lovely to see her confidence and independence beginning to grow.

Hannah could not walk on her own. She could not even stand unsupported when she began school. She had problems with balance and could not get up unaided from a sitting position on the floor. If sitting on a chair, she could lean forward and get herself out of the chair, but was quite likely to propel herself too far and fall onto her face. It was important that her classroom support ensured that Hannah was physically safe whilst allowing her as much independence as possible. This involved a constant balancing act – trying to keep her within reach in case you had to catch her!

As previously mentioned Hannah had splints for her lower legs to support her ankles (ankle-foot orthoses). These were put on top of her socks and were made of plastic moulded to the shape of the sole of her foot and the back of her lower leg. Hannah wore these, held on by velcro and her shoes, throughout her time in Reception with remarkably little complaining. When she began Year 1 Hannah had grown a little, although she was still very small for her age, and she needed to have new leg supports fitted. Unfortunately she had to attend the hospital for this procedure and would not allow the doctor anywhere near her. Her reaction was so bad that it was decided a general anaesthetic was needed for the fitting. This delayed things considerably. In fact Hannah went through most of Years 1 and 2 without any support to her lower legs. This made life easier for the classroom support as it was one less thing to worry about. However, without leg supports Hannah's knees were put under pressure. The physiotherapist explained that she would need new supports fitted at some point to prevent damage in the long-term.

To help her walk around school Hannah had her 'rolator' or 'zimmie'. Hannah's class always occupied the largest classroom in the school to accommodate the 'zimmie' and allow her ease of movement in the class environment. We were also careful to emphasise to the children the importance of keeping their chairs well tucked in to prevent accidents and allow optimum space.

Hannah could walk up to 100 metres with her 'zimmie' with occasional short rest stops. She found it extremely difficult to walk backwards, especially as her 'zimmie' would lock and not allow her this manoeuvre. When she walked towards a door that was closed, she found herself against it, unable to step back to allow the door to open. It was therefore important to be close behind her to be on hand to open doors if required. It was notable that the children soon got used to helping her in this way and allowed her time to get through narrow doorways without pushing to get past. During her time in the infant school, Hannah had the height of her rolator adjusted several times in line with her growth. This was to ensure that she could hold on to it without having to stoop.

I shall never forget my feelings at the beginning of Year 2 when Hannah arrived with a new rolator with a different design. Rather than the frame being in front of Hannah as she walked along, this one had the frame behind her. This meant Hannah had nothing to stop her falling forwards if she decided to step out of her 'zimmie'! I followed her out into the playground that first play time and, as usual, Hannah headed straight for the wooden garden benches at the side of the playground. She stopped her rolator a couple of feet from the arm of the bench but she kept going! Her momentum carried her body forward and her feet could not keep up. I caught her just before her head hit the solid arm of the chair. I explained to her how important it was to stop completely before she let go of her 'zimmie'. It was interesting to note that her family had never had this problem at home because there was not the space to build up that amount of momentum. We talked with Hannah's mother about our concerns that Hannah was going to be vulnerable to accidents at this time. She agreed that a grazed nose and a bleeding knee were a small price to pay for Hannah's developing independence.

Each morning began with the children sitting on the carpet close to the teacher's chair and they returned here several times during the school day. It was therefore important for Hannah to be able to get from sitting on the floor to a standing position. This was very hard for Hannah. At first she needed a hand to help her into a standing position while the rolator, or a piece of furniture, was placed within reach. The physiotherapist, on one of her visits, explained how Hannah should be encouraged to get up on her own. She had to swing her body round so that she was leaning on her hands, then move her legs so that she was on 'all fours' with her feet on the ground and her hands supporting her. She could then gradually remove her hands from the floor transferring her weight onto her feet. It was not until Hannah was in Year 2 that she began to be able to do this. Often she tried the manoeuvre but would 'overthrow' and topple backwards onto her bottom. If she did manage to get to her feet she found it very hard to remain upright and was unable to maintain her balance for more than a second or so. On the few occasions when Hannah did it completely unaided she got a round of applause from her peers!

As Hannah was so small it was not difficult to carry her, however this was done very seldom. It was useful when the fire alarm went off and Hannah could line up quickly with all the others, having been picked up by me. The same was true for swimming lessons in Year 2 when the coach was too far away for Hannah to walk to using her rolator. She could have managed the distance with some rest stops but time was at a premium and we had to keep up with the others. By the end of the walk I needed a long rest! Hannah liked being carried, but used it as a wonderful time to lean in all sorts of directions to wave at her friends. I soon explained to her that whenever she moved her body away from mine, it really hurt my back and that if she did that, I wouldn't be able to carry her. She was immediately very co-operative.

It is important to mention here that I felt happy carrying Hannah as I had been given training, as a nurse, in lifting and carrying. It is essential that such training be given if any lifting is required.

Hannah had great difficulty with balancing and walking so it was very important to ensure she was safe as she made her way around the school. Like all of the children in her class, she had her turn taking the register box to the office. Usually two children went each time: one taking the box and the other holding the register. Hannah joined in this task with enthusiasm and walked holding my hand with the register in the other hand. Sometimes she wanted to carry the box, this meant I had to hold her hand and help support the box, which was too heavy for her to manage on her own. Not an easy task when you are bending down to a child's level as you try and walk along! As the children got more used to Hannah and were able to carry the box using only one hand they would be able to hold her hand and walk with her to the office. It was wonderful to watch Hannah walking down the hall towards the office, holding a friend's hand and carrying the register; in fact doing what all the other children were doing every day. It was especially pleasing to note that I never saw any child, on an occasion like this, hurry Hannah or get impatient with her.

Hannah was moving confidently around the school. She knew what she could and could not manage physically. The next step was to work on her gross motor skills and extend her physical ability. It was time to incorporate the physiotherapy programme into her school curriculum.

Key points

- Spend some time with the child helping them to get to know the layout of the school, so that in time they can find their way around independently.
- Avoid carrying the child; only do so if really necessary. If a child is to be lifted ensure proper training is given in lifting and handling.
- When communicating with the child, try to position yourself so that you are, as far as possible, at the same level. This is particularly important if the child is sitting on the carpet and is unable to get up. This will make your communication clearer and much less threatening.
- Encourage the child to do as much as possible for themselves, even if it takes a long time. It is very easy to do things for them, but it will delay growth in independence.
- Whilst respecting a child's independence, be alert for possible falls.

9 Hannah's physiotherapy programme

Hannah's physiotherapy sessions took place for about fifteen minutes just before lunch on Thursdays. The sessions were in the morning when she was less tired, with the same class-room support helping to ensure consistency for Hannah. The physiotherapy programme was outlined by the physiotherapist who visited approximately once a term to assess Hannah's progress and determine any changes to the regime. We decided that Hannah would do her physiotherapy with one of the children in the class.

The long-term aim of the physiotherapy was to get Hannah walking with the aid of sticks. The first objective was to improve balance in her upper body. After several months of this she would be introduced to the idea of using a support in each hand, rather than a frame, to help her walk.

At 11.45 a.m. I would tell Hannah that it was time for her exercises; she then told her friend (a little boy in the class whom the teachers felt would benefit from some gross motor skills practice). It was important that Hannah was taken out of class for as few activities as possible so that she did not miss work. It was also important that she was seen as a full member of the class. She needed to do what her peers were doing. The boy who came with Hannah loved the experience and soon lots of children were asking to be Hannah's partner.

Our first requirement for these sessions was space. We also needed two large mats, a hoop and a beanbag. Sometimes we were lucky and a small room was available. If not, we did the exercises in a dead-end corridor where very few people would be walking. Hannah and her friend helped collect the equipment. Hannah's task was usually to bring the beanbag. In true Hannah form she soon wanted to be involved in carrying the heavy mats!

Hannah and her friend removed their socks and shoes unaided and sat on the mat waiting for the routine to start. Hannah had a great sense of fairness and signalled for me to take my shoes off as well. This I did. It became a great joke after a while, as Hannah signed to me each time that I had smelly feet! If she ever forgot, her friend reminded her. I noticed that he never dared to say it to me himself but it was a great game to use Hannah as the intermediary.

The first weekly sessions focused on upper-body balance and took place during Year 1. The first stage in the fifteen-minute session was getting Hannah to kneel on the mat and rise up to an upright kneeling position. For several months she needed a supporting hand to stop her toppling over. Her friend would do the same at the other end of the mats. Hannah would then try to walk on her knees towards her friend with minimal help and without toppling over. When she reached him they would shake hands and say, 'How do you do?'. She would then have to try and walk backwards, returning to her place. Going backwards was extremely difficult for her, and at first she could not move at all. Gradually she began to get a small amount of control over that movement, although she could not attempt it without a supporting hand to stop her from over-balancing. This exercise was repeated several times with each child having a turn. I had to make sure Hannah's skirt was tucked into her knickers as it was quite long and impeded her movement.

The next stage was throwing the beanbag to each other. This was done whilst kneeling upright and helped Hannah learn to maintain her balance. It also gave her practice in throwing and catching.

The final exercise involved Hannah trying to balance upright on one knee with the other foot on the floor. She had great difficulty with this at first and needed to have her foot placed on the floor and held there. She was also far from being able to maintain any balance, although this improved slowly. At the end of the session, the children would put their shoes back on, we would return the equipment and go and join the rest of the class on the carpet just before lunch.

The most satisfying aspect of Hannah's physiotherapy came at the beginning of Year 2 when the physiotherapist arrived with two tripods for Hannah. These were two light-weight, stainless steel sticks each with three spread out feet at the bottom to make them more stable. She explained that Hannah's family had had these at home, but there was little open space available there for practice. The bulk of this work therefore would be better done at school. Until this moment I had never realised just how complicated walking was. Did you know that your upper body moves in the opposite direction to your lower limbs when you are walking? That you twist at the hip and swing both parts of your body in different directions for every step? I didn't know this and Hannah certainly didn't know it either. This was going to be a challenge!

The first task was to introduce Hannah to her new tripods and explain that she was going to practice walking with these and that one day she could use something very similar to these instead of her frame. This meant she would be able to go backwards and get through much narrower spaces. As always, Hannah was willing to have a go.

The physiotherapist explained that, at first, Hannah needed to be able to stand upright using the tripods as support. This was easy for her. The next stage was to be able to lift up the tripods in turn without falling over. This took practice. Then came the tricky part. Hannah had to learn to lift up the tripod in her right hand and at the same time lift her left foot to take a step. She then had to move her left foot and right tripod forward a step and place them on the ground whilst putting her weight on her right leg and on the tripod in her left hand. She could then transfer her weight forward and repeat the movement using the opposite leg and tripod. The physiotherapist gave me some little bits of bright red and blue paper. These helped us remember which tripod to move with which foot.

This stage of Hannah's physiotherapy was very complicated so we decided that she should do this on her own, with no distractions. She did not therefore have another child with her; but children walking past were very interested in what she was doing and often had to be persuaded to go back to their own classroom.

When it was time for this physiotherapy, Hannah and I collected her two tripods which were kept in the corner of the classroom. We also got the four precious pieces of coloured paper. We were now ready and only needed some clear floor space. I stuck one of the red pieces of paper on to one of the tripods. The other red piece I placed on the top of her right shoe, held on by the velcro strap, and easily visible to Hannah. The blue paper was then stuck to the other tripod and placed in the same way on her left foot. It was important always to put the same colours on the same feet so as to confuse Hannah as little as possible. I used to remember 'Red goes on Right'. I would then help Hannah stand up.

It was at times like these that I had to make a decision. Hannah could probably manage to stand up by herself with a lot of time and effort. I decided it was more important for her to have energy to concentrate on the difficult manoeuvre of walking with sticks and so I helped her stand up.

Once Hannah was standing, I stood behind her and we looked down at her shoes. I pointed to the red and blue markers. I then put the red tripod in her left hand, to coincide with her red-right foot. I then put the blue tripod in her right hand to coincide with her left foot. I then explained that we were going to lift the red ones, foot and tripod, off the ground together and move them forward a little way. It was important that they were moved to the side and not directly in front of Hannah's other foot. Once we had moved the red ones, I helped Hannah to move the blue ones together, again keeping them to the side but not so far away that they failed to support her.

As we moved each tripod, I reminded Hannah to move the correct foot. At first she moved any foot and I would say 'Remember Hannah. Blue tripod – blue foot.' I always said, 'Red. . .blue. . .red. . .blue. . .red. . .blue' as she tried to walk along, with me behind her holding and supporting her.

As the weeks went by, Hannah became very familiar with her red and blue bits of paper and always knew which foot to put them on. She was able to attach them to her shoes herself. Eventually I was to stand in front of Hannah, instead of directly behind her, while she tried walking. I still had to remind her which colour came next, to put the tripods out to the side and not to obstruct her other foot.

I remember the day when Hannah stood, balanced with her tripods. I said 'Start with red' and she moved her red foot and red tripod forward without me telling her or indicating directly which ones to move. It was a wonderful moment and such a contrast to the little girl months before, who had very little control over these tripods and whose legs and arms were going all over the place.

There was still a lot of work to do. Hannah could place her feet correctly to take one or two steps, but then she tried going too fast or lost her concentration. It was at this stage that the physiotherapist brought along the next set of 'sticks' for Hannah to use. These were not made of metal with three legs as the tripods were. They were made of wood and were as tall as Hannah with a square piece of flat wood on the bottom, to make contact with the floor. They were less stable and would mean Hannah was maintaining more of her balance herself. Hannah was to grip them where it felt comfortable and walk in the way she had practised with the tripods. We got our pieces of red and blue paper, stuck them on and were ready for this next stage.

Hannah had a few weeks of practice with her sticks before the end of the summer term and her move to the Junior School. Once again she worked hard and learned how to use them. She learned how to get up off the floor whilst using her sticks for support, and how to place her weight as she tried to walk. It was really beginning to come together when the summer holidays came.

There was more work to do before Hannah would be ready for the move to using sticks instead of her cumbersome frame, but she was progressing and there seemed every chance that this would be her way of mobilising in the future.

That is perhaps what characterised Hannah's mobility. It was a struggle for her to stand unsupported, get up from sitting on the floor, kneel unsupported, or move backwards. She could manage well with her frame as long as she did not have to manoeuvre a slope or stairs, go backwards or open a door. Yet she persevered. She never gave up. She would always have a go, unless she was completely exhausted, and she was always thrilled with her successes.

These successes did come. Slowly but surely progress could be seen and gradually Hannah showed us that, given time, she could improve in her gross motor skills and surprise us all.

Key points

- Don't be afraid to display boundless enthusiasm for what may seem like the smallest of achievements.
- Keep physical exercises and routines simple and repetitive so that the child knows what to expect.
- Involve other class members in activities whenever possible.
- Take regular advice from the qualified physiotherapist.
- Make physiotherapy fun for you and the child.
- Stick to regular and set times for the session.

10 Eating, drinking and using the toilet

Hannah loved her food. During her half-term spent in the Reception class, she went home at 12.00 and so did not stay for lunch. She stayed for one full day on the exciting occasion of the Reception classes' outing to a local park for a picnic and kite flying. I sat next to Hannah on the bus, armed with her frame, her buggy (this occasionally came to school when an outing involved too much walking), her personalised kite made in class, and a bag with a change of clothing in case of accidents. Hannah was in charge of the carrier bag containing her packed lunch. If she showed me the contents of her packed lunch once, she showed it to me 18 times during that journey! She could hardly contain her excitement and could focus on little else.

Hannah stayed for lunch from the beginning of Year 1. Her mother always gave her the same lunch. It was finger food, easy for her to eat and suited her well. She would have Cheddar cheese sandwiches, cut up into mouth size pieces, some snacks and loose raisins in a small bag and a banana.

Hannah's lunch box was kept in a plastic bag which she left each morning on the trolley in the corridor with all the other lunch boxes. At lunch time she walked with the other children to the trolley, using her 'zimmie'. At first she needed help to get her lunch-box and hang it on the handle of her frame so that she could walk with it into lunch. By the end of Year 2 she would walk out with her frame, sit herself down beside the trolley, find her lunchbox (often the other children had already grabbed theirs so there was only hers left) and painstakingly hang the plastic bag's handles over the frame handle. This often took two or three attempts as one handle would slip off as she attempted to position the other. She persevered and would stand up with the help of the frame. She was then ready to walk into lunch and join her friends.

Very often Hannah was 'bagged' by one of her friends who saved a seat for her at the table. We asked that Hannah always sat on one of the end seats. This was to ensure easy access to her as she could sometimes choke on her food. This was usually caused by Hannah pushing too many sandwiches into her mouth. The choking was easily remedied by removing all the food in her mouth using a finger, together with lots of calm reassurance. It could be quite distressing for Hannah and those children close by, so it was important to be within easy reach should she have this problem.

She was independent in her eating in most other respects, although she made rather a mess of the floor and table close by her. She indicated when she was ready to peel her banana and I started it for her and held it while she pulled each piece of peel off. This meant she held the skinless banana in her hand while she ate it. The result was a lot of soft, liquid banana on her hands, lips and chin and quite often on her sweatshirt! It was interesting that on these occasions she did not mind the feeling of mess on her hands.

When Hannah was ready to eat her 'raisin pudding' she lifted up the plastic bag and emptied the raisins onto the table. She then ate them one by one, picking them up using her kind of pincer grip, using the side of her thumb and the side of her first finger, close to the knuckle. We encouraged her to use a more conventional pincer grip using the tips of her thumb and first finger. This was to encourage her fine motor control. It was hard for her and, especially if she was very hungry, she would stick to the 'Hannah' approach, which was quicker and took less concentration.

Hannah found lunch time a delightful experience. She always had friends around her whose food she found most interesting. She quickly learned the routine of putting up her hand for more water from the dinner ladies or if she was ready to go. She developed a game with one of the dinner ladies who pretended each day to steal and hide her banana. Hannah then got it back and in return gave her dinner lady imaginary bananas, sometimes counting up to ten of them.

Hannah was slow at eating her lunch. If her class was 'first sitting' she would still be eating when the 'second sitting' came in. We tried to speed her up so that she did not miss too much of her play time. I think that she really loved the hustle and bustle of lunch time and the chance to see lots of children from different classes.

When she finished eating, I wiped Hannah's face and fingers with the paper towel her mother always included. It was details like this that made it so easy to look after Hannah when she had slightly different needs from the other children. Sometimes Hannah was so messy that she needed to be washed at the basin. Her sweatshirt sometimes got a lot of banana on it, but we made a conscious decision not to give her a bib. We just mopped up any mess and changed her top if necessary. After lunch it was time to get some play and Hannah returned her lunchbox to the trolley. On the way out she passed the dinner ladies serving puddings to the children. She always stopped and looked longingly at their food.

Lunch time was an important social time for Hannah. She responded to the other children who often helped her open the stiff lid of her lunchbox and were eager to show her the contents of their boxes. There was no doubt that Hannah was a messy eater, but her classmates accepted this and were keen to help her and sit next to her. Only once did a child say that he did not want to sit next to Hannah at lunch time, but even his feelings changed as he got used to her.

The speech and language therapist wanted Hannah to work on her tongue control. It was suggested that I encourage Hannah to use her tongue, rather than her fingers, to move food around her mouth. She was also reminded to close her mouth as she ate. This had the added advantage of making eating less messy for her.

Drinking was also quite messy for Hannah. At milk time she brought in her own beaker with a lid and two handles and had goat's milk from home to drink. Hannah managed this well, although milk would seep out the sides of her mouth and down her chin. When she sat with her friends, I placed a box of tissues on the table and the friends willingly mopped up Hannah and any mess left on the table. This was when I took my morning break and it was good to see the children filling the gap and helping Hannah appropriately in my absence.

If Hannah needed a drink of water at play time she had to be lifted up for her mouth to reach the water fountain. On some hot days she was very thirsty and it was hard work holding her in position. I then showed Hannah how she could, with help, step up on to one of the bars of her frame and balance on that while she had her drink. I always stayed by her side. This worked well.

Going to the toilet became a special event for Hannah and me. We shared many jokes at this time and Hannah was always eager to engage in a chat. It was also a time when I spoke to her about her feelings. Was she finding the work hard? Was it difficult not being able to speak? Did she get cross about things at school? Hannah was usually so uncomplaining and co-operative that if she was upset it was usually very evident. A visit to the toilet was a time when we had privacy and could explore issues that may have been upsetting her.

Hannah signed to me when she needed to go to the toilet. Very occasionally, usually because I had not 'listened' carefully enough to Hannah, she had an accident and wet her pants. On these occasions I quickly whisked her into the toilet and got her a change of clothes. When Hannah's third brother, Yoni, was born, she had a few such accidents which no doubt reflected the changes going on in her home life.

Hannah usually used her frame to walk to the toilet, knowing I would see her in there in a minute. By the end of Year 2 she was very nearly independent in this area. She positioned her frame by the toilet door, supporting herself on the doorframe as she walked into the toilet. I then squeezed in after her, and she pushed the door too. There was no lock on the infant toilet doors. She always used the same toilet as a handle had been positioned on the wall to help steady her as she pulled her pants down and when she was sitting on the toilet. The other children saw her toilet as exclusively hers. No one had ever said anything to them, but they knew which one she used and that it had a special handle. I heard one little girl say, 'You can't use that. It's Hannah's.' This was said in a protective way, as if she were looking after Hannah's interests. I explained that anyone could use it; not just Hannah.

It was agonising to watch her pull up her skirt or dress and try to tuck it under her chin while she held onto the handle with one hand. She then tried to get her fingers to pull down one side of her pants at a time; as she pulled down one side and tried to stretch over to pull down the other side, the first side would slip back up! It took Hannah two years to be able to do this and I remember the first time she managed to get her pants pulled down to her knees without any help. I was so excited and started clapping madly, saying, 'Hannah! How wonderful!' She was quite used to me being rather loud and eccentric and usually found it greatly amusing.

Hannah used a small step that had to be positioned for her to get up onto the toilet. She steadied herself with the handle and could turn round on the step and lower herself onto the toilet seat. Hannah made a good attempt at wiping herself with toilet paper while she was still sitting. If she had opened her bowels she needed help with this and just leaned forward for me to wipe her. Latterly she could get down from the step on her own as long as her knickers had not fallen down to her ankles and stopped her! Once again Hannah struggled to get her knickers back up. At this stage I often helped, as she was tired from all her concentrated attempts at independence. All that was left to do was flush the toilet. It was a stiff flush and Hannah was not strong enough to do it at first. With perseverance, she managed it on her own one day and this was another cause of great celebration for us both!

Hannah left the toilet, washed and dried her hands and returned to the classroom. In Year 1, with her old frame, she always needed me to wait while she did this as she needed help to lift her frame up a small step in order to leave the toilet. The advantage of her new frame was that Hannah could lift it up herself and manoeuvre the step independently. This meant I would meet her back in the classroom when she had finished. Once or twice she seemed to be taking rather a long time. It was usually because she felt she had done enough work for the time being and was having a little rest in the toilet.

As Hannah's independence in the toilet slowly grew, I found I did not need to be in with her the whole time. Once she had sat down I would go and stand outside and watch her over the top of the door. She was most bewildered by this at first and kept beckoning me back in. I explained that she would be fine and I would come back in when she was ready to step down, in case she fell.

Hannah took much longer than her classmates to go to the toilet. I worried that she missed play time or work in the classroom. It slowly dawned on me that, for Hannah, being independent in the toilet was one of her most important learning objectives. If we took 20 minutes in the toilet with her slowly mastering the skill of taking her own pants down, we achieved an enormous amount.

The poetry appreciation would have to wait for another day.

Key points

- Stay close at hand during meal times if the child is vulnerable to choking.
- Don't worry about messy eating and drinking. It can always be cleared up later and it is very important to promote independence in this area.
- Avoid using a bib as it draws unnecessary attention to the child.
- As far as possible, find ways for the child to do what the other children do, e.g. collecting and returning their own lunchbox, putting up their hand to tell you they are ready to go.
- Recognise that mid-morning break and lunch time are important social times for the children and be as unobtrusive as possible. The presence of an adult will fundamentally change the nature of any social interaction.
- Be straightforward and direct when helping the child in the toilet. Try not to show any embarrassment as it will immediately be noticed and may distract the child.

11 Will you be my friend?

In school, children work on reading, writing, maths and much more but there is one subject that can make or break a child's school life – friendships.

How was Hannah, who was unable to speak or walk unaided, going to make and keep friends? When children were skipping and running in the playground, how could we ensure that Hannah was not left out and become isolated? Children can be cruel. Supposing she was teased? She may well have been on the same reading level as many of her friends, and be able to access her computer with more ease than many adults, but what happened if she made no friends – and became sad?

It is important to look at how staff responded to Hannah as this had a great effect on her peers.

Hannah was different and she was special – but so were the other 29 children in her class. At the beginning we found it terribly hard to tell Hannah off. It seemed cruel to be stern with someone who looked so fragile and little. But this was to be a real school experience. In the mornings, the children came into the class, having put away their lunchboxes and coats, and settled on the carpet in front of the teacher. This was a time for the children to be quiet. Hannah was always happy to see her classmates and started each day with great enthusiasm. However, the children were expected not to talk so that the register could be taken and instructions for the day's work talked through. If Hannah tried to distract her neighbour during this carpet time she was told off. If she took her shoes off she was told not to be silly and they were firmly put back on.

There was not enough time on a Monday morning for all of the 30 children to tell their news and if Hannah had news she had to wait her turn like the others. If she was chosen, we then encouraged her signing and vocalisation and reinforced her signing by talking to the class. We knew her news from checking the home-school diary. If Hannah had produced a lovely piece of work, she showed it to the rest of her class, but no more often than her peers. Hannah was one child in 30 in Yellow Room and one child in 230 in Trafalgar Infant School, and that is how her peers saw her. This was important because her friends could reassure their parents that having Hannah back for tea or taking her to the cinema was, in fact, not a daunting task. She was just like them.

For the first two terms, at the start of each school day, Hannah's mother brought her into the class from the playground. It was reassuring for us to be able to have a quick chat with her mother and for her to know that Hannah was happily settled in. But as time went on it was important for Hannah and her peers that she was doing the same as them. We discussed with Hannah, her mother and the class as a whole, that it would be nice for the children from Yellow Room to bring her in themselves. We explained that when they saw her in the morning and the bell had gone, they could collect her from her mother, along with her reading folder and lunch box, and bring her into class. She was never short of helpers and arrived in the class smiling and laughing.

Two children from the class list were chosen each day to be Hannah's helpers. They took her into Assembly and were responsible for calling for one of the classroom assistants if they were needed. From there they took Hannah to the classroom to collect her 'zimmie', took her out to play and accompanied her back to class. There was only one child who found it hard to help Hannah; it was this boy's insecurity and lack of confidence that formed this barrier. He was never unkind to her, and would never have hurt her, but due to his own lack of self worth, he felt unable to give Hannah the support she needed. Hannah sensed this and resisted help from him. No pressure was put on him and both children were happy to politely ignore one another.

Children are not generally patronising. Hannah's peers warmed to her because of her kindness and sense of humour. They benefited from her presence by developing patience and empathy and dampening their usual egocentric approach. As we encouraged Hannah's independence, her friendships formed naturally. Play time gave Hannah the opportunity to mix with other children, without the immediate presence of an adult. It was here that we became very aware of the importance of stepping back while still making sure she was emotionally and physically safe. We encouraged the children to learn the signs Hannah commonly used so that they could communicate with her on their own. It is easier and more natural for children to form friendships and relationships without the close supervision of an adult.

Once out in the playground, Hannah would sit on a bench or on the ground and would be joined by her regular friends or children from other classes. Even though she was so popular, she was not fussed over. The naturalness of these relationships showed itself when other children were quite comfortable in saying to Hannah, 'No, I don't want to play with

Figure 13 Hannah with her playmates

you today'. Whilst always keeping an eye out for Hannah, we would spend play time walking around talking to other children and sorting out playground scraps and tiffs. Hannah was happy to sit and listen to the other children talking or play some favourite signing games, which her friends learnt. Most children in the school had learnt Hannah's 'ice-cream' and 'doctor' games referred to in Chapter 5 and Hannah was pleased to play them with a selection of friends and not just her Classroom Support.

One of Hannah's real favourites was an old playground chant: 'Who stole the cookie from the cookie jar?' A group of children would sit in a circle with one of them hiding the 'cookie' and start chanting and signing:

Who stole the cookie from the cookie jar?	The children chose a child and pointed.
Hannah stole the cookie from the cookie jar Who me?	Hannah shook her head.
Couldn't be Then who?	Hannah pointed.
Amber stole the cookie from the cookie jar	Amber would show the cookie.

When all the children were kept in the class because it was raining, Hannah coped with the inevitable chaos and noise that you would expect from 30 lively children. She would sit with a group and draw, or share a book. Whilst we would be there to monitor her safety she would cheekily take advantage of her play time freedom and crawl from one activity to another – crawling was something she was not supposed to do. Her friends loved seeing Hannah being 'naughty' and would sign and say, 'Hannah – you're being cheeky'. The sign for cheeky is a gentle pull of the cheek.

Hannah did not like to see any of her friends or schoolmates being upset. If she saw someone crying she would shuffle on her bottom to be by their side and put her arms round them. Her own empathy and kindness were very natural, warm and comforting. Hannah's dinner lady, Mrs Wells, once said, 'Hannah is popular, not because of her problems but because she is such a nice little girl.'

She soon started going out to tea and having invitations to parties. Hannah loved going to friends or having them to her house. It was not uncommon for her to suddenly start signing who she was going to have tea with in the middle of a maths lesson! She was told that we would talk about it later. The children saw it as a perfectly normal thing to do, and it was they who understood Hannah's signing and what she did and didn't like. Hannah's mother liased with the friend's mother to reassure them. The only difference on those afternoons was that Hannah's mother brought her buggy into school so that it was easy to take her back to her friend's house.

Hannah had many friends but, like all young children, she had some best friends. One of them, Laura, wrote this and drew a picture of them both together.

Laura's mother writes:

When I first saw Hannah at school, I couldn't quite decide how I felt. I was worried that she would find school life more difficult than 'normal' kids, and that the kids themselves could make her life difficult if they were cruel. With this in mind, I took Laura to the side to explain that, yes, Hannah was different, but only on the outside.

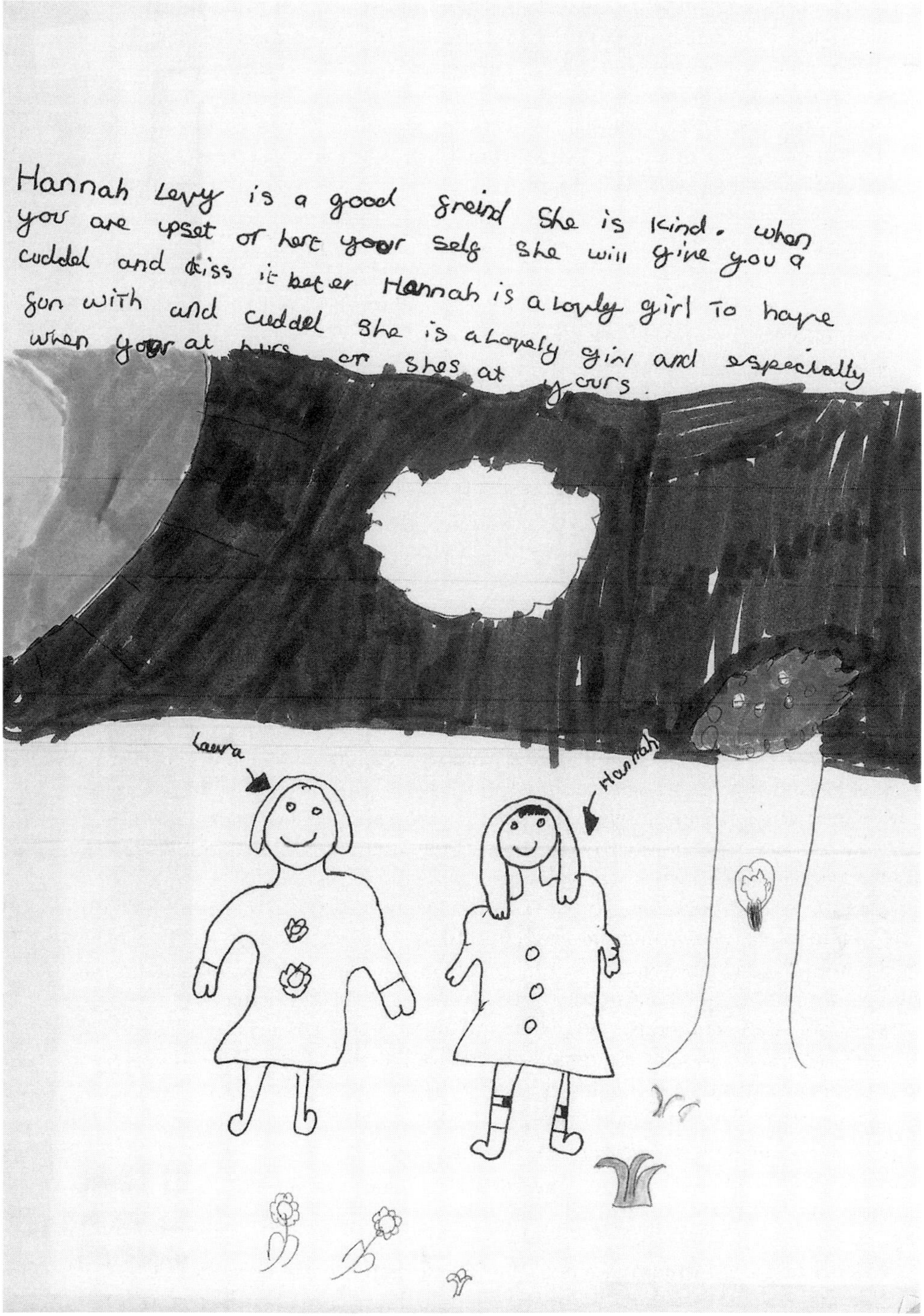

Hannah Levy is a good freind She is Kind. when you are upset or hert your self she will give you a cuddel and kiss it beter Hannah is a lovly girl To have fun with and cuddel she is a Lovely girl and especially when your at hurs or shes at yours.

Figure 14 Laura writes and draws about her friend Hannah

On the inside she felt happy and sad, had good days and bad, and like all of us, would be very hurt if people were not nice to her. Laura quickly grasped that Hannah may need help physically but she also needed friends like everyone else.

Time passed and everyone settled down into groups of friends with Laura and Hannah being partners at school. Friends changed weekly, came for tea and disappeared again. Then Laura asked me could Hannah come for tea? I gently explained that although I liked Hannah very much, I was unable to communicate with her. What if she got upset and I didn't know why? What if she wanted to go upstairs? What could she eat? Would she choke?

My five-year-old daughter then told me in no uncertain terms that I was guilty of treating Hannah differently – exactly what I had told her *not* to do. I felt so ashamed of myself.

I chatted through my worries with Hannah's mum, and later that week Hannah came to tea. I needn't have worried at all. If Hannah wanted something, she'd find a way of letting me know! She was up and down stairs on her tummy like a toddler. No, she didn't choke, and boy does she like chocolate ice-cream!

Hannah is one of Laura's closest friends, and a frequent visitor to our home. She slept over recently with six other girls for Laura's birthday, and was still having fun when the rest had fallen asleep.

The first time she came home was scary, but I'm so pleased that my daughter put me right about treating her differently. Not only has Laura made a much-loved friend, I like to think that Hannah's mum, and indeed the whole family, will be valued friends in the future.

A little girl invited Hannah to a disco party one Saturday in her class. She was excited when she saw her invitation and there was a buzz of excitement around the class when news got out that there was to be a disco. When we heard that her parents were unable to go, and as my own eight-year-old daughter was invited to the same party, I took Hannah. I picked her up from her home and can remember a great feeling of responsibility and a little nervousness as her mother lifted her into the car and I put her 'zimmie' in the boot. She looked so different in her party clothes compared to her school uniform. She sat at the long tables enjoying tea with the other party guests. I cut up the sandwiches and cakes into tiny cubes so that Hannah could stay as clean as possible. As the strobe lighting and loud music started, I waited for Hannah's frightened reaction and prepared to take her out of the hall; but she loved it and wanted to dance. The other children came to dance with her, gently holding her hands to support her.

Hannah loved going to other children's swimming parties and had several of these for her own birthday celebrations. These were probably the only parties when Hannah was accompanied by one of her parents.

In Year 2 Hannah became a Brownie. Her mother talked of the 'normality' of sharing the Brownie Run. Once again Hannah was 'just one of the girls'.

Her Brownie Leader, Linda Hicks of the 16th Twickenham Pack, shared her thoughts about having Hannah as a Brownie.

Hannah has been coming to Brownies for over six months now and she really enjoys it. When she first started she used her zimmer frame a lot and seemed unaware of what was going on. As the weeks have gone on she walks into the hall with a great big smile on her face and points to all her friends. We have no knowledge of sign language which is a problem. When she wants something we have to ask one of the other children, who have learnt sign language at school with her, what she wants. When Hannah became enrolled she signed her promise with mum's help. All the other children have accepted Hannah. She does need quite a bit of help; at the moment the Brownies are working for their craft badge and we are seeing whether we can get special badges for her.

Her favourite game is 'Mouse is creeping'. One child sits on a chair, blindfolded – she is the cat – and the other children sit round in a circle – they are the mice. One of them is chosen and she has to walk around the outside of the of the circle, creeping as quietly as possible so they make no sound. When the cat hears a

Figure 15 Hannah and Laura – enrolled Brownies

sound she points and if right, the creeping mouse becomes the cat. Hannah loves being the cat. She flings her glasses off and happily puts the blindfold on – something she was not happy to do at the beginning. Hannah has been swimming with us and has joined in picnics. She loves being with us and we love having her.

When she was officially 'enrolled' Hannah came to school one morning with her Brownie uniform to show and was thrilled to sign the Brownie promise in front of the whole class.

Hannah was having a wonderful time, experiencing situations that seemed improbable a year before. But it was not just she who was benefiting from being in a mainstream school. All the children and adults in the school learnt how much Hannah had to give. They were able to enjoy the friendship she gave, whilst watching her blossom.

Key points

- Find a path between ensuring the child feels emotionally and physically safe and allowing them to develop and maintain friendships without the close supervision of an adult.
- Encourage those friendships to develop outside school hours; help parents to share concerns.
- Spend time in the playground, particularly in the beginning, teaching groups of children some of the commonly-used signs.
- Appoint different children each day to be the child's helpers.

- Do not make excessive allowances for inappropriate behaviour; do not be afraid to reprimand the child.
- If a child is reluctant to interact with the child with special needs do not put any pressure on them and ensure they do not feel any guilt.

12 Day-to-day learning

Hannah was secure, happy and her independence was developing. Everything was in place for her to learn and to extend her academic skills. Hannah's specialist teacher set out the structure and objectives for Hannah's learning. With the support of the SENCO and class teachers, we implemented this programme. In some areas she progressed at a steady rate and in other areas she became stuck. We sought professional advice when this happened, but it was important to remember that Hannah, like all children, experienced plateaux of learning. She never appeared to become frustrated or disillusioned when she found work hard; in fact it was us, her classroom supports, who had to be reassured that all was going well and not to worry that she was struggling to reach an Individual Educational Plan (IEP) target. Hannah worked alongside her classmates covering the same curriculum. The work, however, was differentiated to allow a more realistic access to what was being taught.

We ensured her time was divided between working one-to-one with her classroom support or class teacher, working with a group of children and working on her own. Hannah's concentration span was less than that of her peers so we made sure the day was broken into 10-to-20 minute sessions, with some 'time out' between these. It is important to recognise that a child receiving one-to-one support, particularly full-time, can be given an intense workload. When we were working with Hannah she could not drift off into a daydream or secretly chat with her neighbour, a privilege that her classmates had.

Hannah remained in the classroom for her work unless we needed more space or on rare occasions when she needed to work without the noise of the classroom. Following an assessment by CENMAC (Centre for Micro-Assisted Communication), the Local Education Authority (LEA) generously provided Hannah with a RM Window Box™ Personal Computer. This was a turning point for her and enabled us to ensure she could work to her full potential across all areas of the curriculum. She could work at her own pace and her confidence was enhanced as she could access different programmes independently.

One area that I found difficult as classroom support was working with Hannah within a group of children who were all, in their own way, demanding of extra support. On one occasion I was asked by the class teacher to be with such a group for a practical maths session. Hannah's special needs teacher, who was acting in her consultancy role, was observing this session. We played a game that consisted of throwing dice and moving counters around a board. One child insisted on throwing the dice so hard it went to the other side of the class, another moved the counter six times even though he had only thrown a 2, another started crying, and one was enthusiastic to play. Hannah took great delight in putting the counters in her lap. Nobody benefited and I was reduced to tears. I realised that although it was very important for Hannah to work with other children, it was essential to find a group of children that she could work with who were at more or less the same level, but who were not constantly demanding individual attention.

Numeracy

One important aspect of Hannah's curriculum was numeracy. It is worth mentioning here that she attended the infant school prior to the implementation of the National Numeracy Strategy. In Year 1 we became concerned that Hannah was not achieving a basic understanding of number. We were comparing her to her peers and finding their understanding was far more advanced. Literature from the Down Syndrome Educational Trust in Portsmouth proved to be invaluable. (The Trust exists to advance the development and education of children and adults with Down's syndrome and conducts scientific research into their developmental difficulties and how they may be most effectively educated.)

When working on numeracy with Hannah, we often had to repeat work to reinforce the skills she was acquiring, whilst ensuring that boredom did not creep in. We did this by approaching the work in slightly different ways; either by changing the form of the number task or exercise or by moving from paired to individual work. In this way she benefited from a varied access to the curriculum and we hope we reduced the boredom factor.

One of our first tasks was to ensure that Hannah recognised the numbers 0 to 10 and then on to 20 and that she could sequence them. We printed the numbers 0 to 20 onto coloured board, laminated them and then cut them into two-inch squares. Hannah would sit on the floor and she would find 0, 1, 2, 3 and so on and put them into the right order. When she had finished the sequencing we would ask her to give us back, for example, 12, 17, 9 ensuring she recognised the numbers out of order.

The computer came into its own when it came to independent maths work. There was one particular programme, 'Numberpics Count'™, which was invaluable, but which had to be used carefully so that Hannah remained interested. There were two ways of using the programme – 'counting' and 'finding'. For the 'counting' section, a picture showing one to ten objects was displayed on the screen. At the same time, beneath the picture, buttons appeared, which were labelled '1', '2', and so on up to '10'. Hannah counted up the number of objects and then pressed the relevant number button (see figure 16).

For 'Find', four pictures were displayed on the screen simultaneously. Each picture had a different number of objects on it and a numeral from '1' to '10' placed in the centre of the screen. Hannah had to match the correct set of objects with the corresponding numeral (see figure 17).

This programme allowed Hannah to record her answers. These could then be printed off so we could monitor her progress whilst allowing her to work independently. She would work on this either on her own, with a classmate, which encouraged her turn taking skills, or with an adult. It was easy to know when Hannah was getting bored with this programme – she would simply put silly answers down or exit and enter one of her favourite programmes.

Hannah was very familiar with the game of dominoes. She played this at least once a week in the class using large-sized dominoes. This helped reinforce her number recognition. It was interesting that there were several children who did not know the game. They benefited from learning it and playing it with Hannah. She took great delight in correcting a move if her partner had made a mistake. The large-sized dominoes were ideal for this situation.

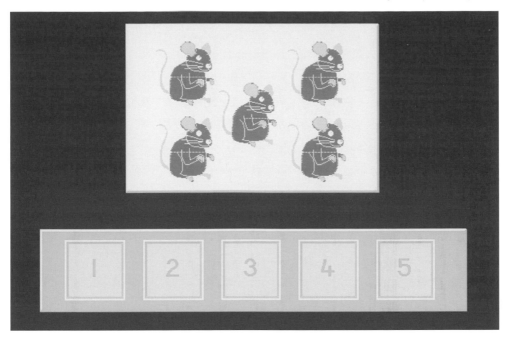

Figure 16 Numberpics – Count

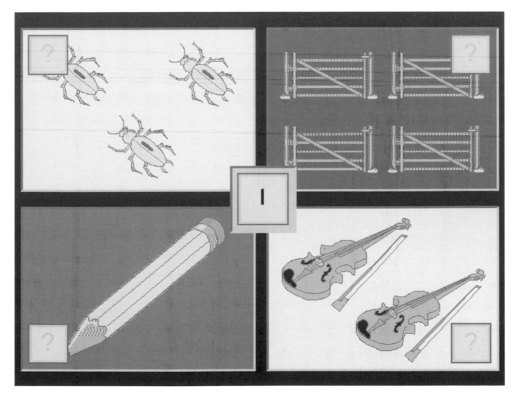

Figure 17 Numberpics – Find

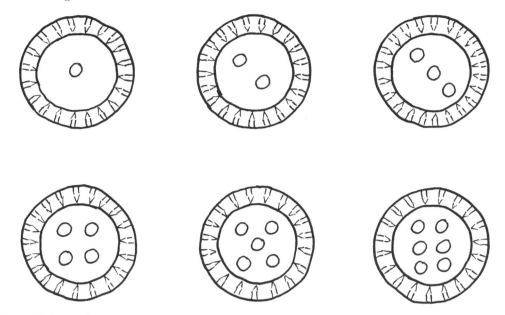

Figure 18 Paper plate counting game

Another game we played involved two players having six paper plates each with one to six circles in them.

The children took turns in throwing the dice. When the number came up, the player counted into the relevant plate the correct number of counters (they became chocolates, ice-creams or biscuits – whatever took Hannah's fancy). The winner was the person to fill all their plates first.

These were all practical games, which allowed Hannah to grasp and make sense of mathematical concepts. Throwing dice, picking up counters and playing dominoes also allowed Hannah to work on her fine motor skills.

Literacy

At home Hannah grew up surrounded by books. She had a great love of them and this followed her into school, where her reading skills were on a level with her peers. In fact, it was the one area in which she actually surpassed some of her classmates.

The reading system at Trafalgar Infant School was strongly supported by a home reading scheme. The children changed their books daily, if they needed to, and only asked for help if they were changing sets, levels or couldn't find the right book. The children read their book once a week in the class and were encouraged to read daily at home. Hannah was introduced to this system when she started.

Every morning Hannah went into the school hall at the allotted time and changed her reading book. In Year 1 her classroom support went with her but by Year 2 she was able to go with a friend. Hannah could change her book on her own, but had problems negotiating her 'zimmie' and holding the book at the same time. She often took the books from her set and spread them out around her so that she could choose more easily. She enjoyed being in the hall with her friends, surrounded by books, and would occasionally have to be reminded not to take all day about it!

We read with her three times a week and, like the other children in the class, she read to the class teacher once a week, which she loved. She sat next to the teacher on the teacher's chair looking very pleased with herself. Reading with a child who cannot speak was an interesting experience. From Hannah's mother we learnt a method of hearing her read in two stages. First she looked at the pictures and vocalised. She then turned the pages, pointed to the words and vocalised sounds that matched the number of words on a page. She became very animated at times and her enjoyment and expressions indicated to us that she understood what she was reading. We then went back to the start of the book and Hannah signed through the story. If we came to a word that we didn't know, we referred to our Makaton Vocabulary book; it was an ideal opportunity for us all to learn new signs.

The children enjoyed paired reading once a week. They were put with partners of similar abilities and interests and shared their books. They sat for fifteen minutes and their time was divided between reading and listening. Hannah loved hearing her partner, Laura, read and when it came to Hannah's turn, we spent some of that time reading the book out loud while she signed. Laura was keen to be Hannah's partner; they were very close friends and Laura understood her well and would take no nonsense from her. If Hannah tried to sign about Shabbat, ice-creams or another favourite subject in the middle of this session, Laura told her and signed, in no uncertain terms, that this was reading time and she could save her chatting for play time. Hannah then got back to the task in hand.

Although Hannah loved reading and responded to the text, we couldn't be sure how much she understood. Hannah loved Oxford Reading Tree's Biff; Chip and Kipper books and the vocabulary of these books lent itself very well to signing and simple comprehension questions. Some examples are outlined here from one of Hannah's favourite books, *The Babysitter*©.

Biff was hungry.

They made a sandwich.

Figure 19 Extract from *The Babysitter*

- Was Biff hungry?
- Did Biff make a sandwich or a cake?
- How many mugs are on the table?
- Does the babysitter look happy or cross?
- How do the children look?
- What is Chip holding in his hand?

It was very difficult to assess her comprehension capabilities and Hannah's specialist teacher devised a more formal system of assessing her understanding (Appendix 8). This type of assessment was used successfully at half-termly intervals.

We also used a game 'Make a Scene – Spot'™, bought from a local supermarket, which reinforced Hannah's understanding and helped develop her abstract thinking. The game involved moveable vinyl shapes, which were placed on a laminated playboard. We asked Hannah to place certain characters and objects in different positions; it was a fun way to ensure she understood the meaning of 'on', 'next to', 'under', etc.

The Literacy Hour was slowly introduced during the summer term of Year 2. For the first fifteen minutes, the children, as a class, shared a Big Book together. Hannah enjoyed this and read the story with the other children. When it came to looking at different concepts, e.g. rhyming or punctuation, she became bored and fidgety. She needed her one-to-one support for these more complex areas and her time was more beneficially spent away from class teaching, working in this way.

Spelling was another important skill for Hannah to learn and the computer was again very useful for this area of the curriculum. The school used a system called CAT (Correct All the Time) spellings, which was introduced several years ago by one of the teachers. The words were based on those most commonly read and used by the children. The spellings were divided into groups for Year 1 and Year 2. Hannah concentrated on Year 1 spellings over both school years. When the rest of the class were having their spelling practice we sat at the computer and went through Hannah's list. I said and signed a word and Hannah typed it into the computer. I was impressed on several occasions by how hard Hannah worked and the amount of effort that she put into everything she did. She not only had to think of the spelling but she then had to put physical effort into pressing the right key on the keyboard. She never complained. We then printed off her spellings, making any corrections and she would show the class teacher her work (see figure 20).

I then helped her stick them into her spelling book. If we were away from the computer she would finger spell to show how to spell a word, although with her lack of fine motor control she was not always able to be very accurate. She always managed 'a' as it used her thumb and was therefore easier to differentiate, but the other vowels were rather hit and miss!

Handwriting

Hannah found it difficult to exert any fine control over her hand movements. This made handwriting very hard for her. She was also left-handed which had implications for the way that the paper was placed on the desk. When she first came into Reception and the class were doing handwriting, I tried to get her to practice one or two letters, usually 'a' and 'c'. The difficulty was that the children were being taught cursive, or joined-up writing, and Hannah found the extra links involved too complicated. After checking with the class teacher, we decided to concentrate on helping Hannah to write a recognisable letter and not to worry about any links. Having practised her writing while being

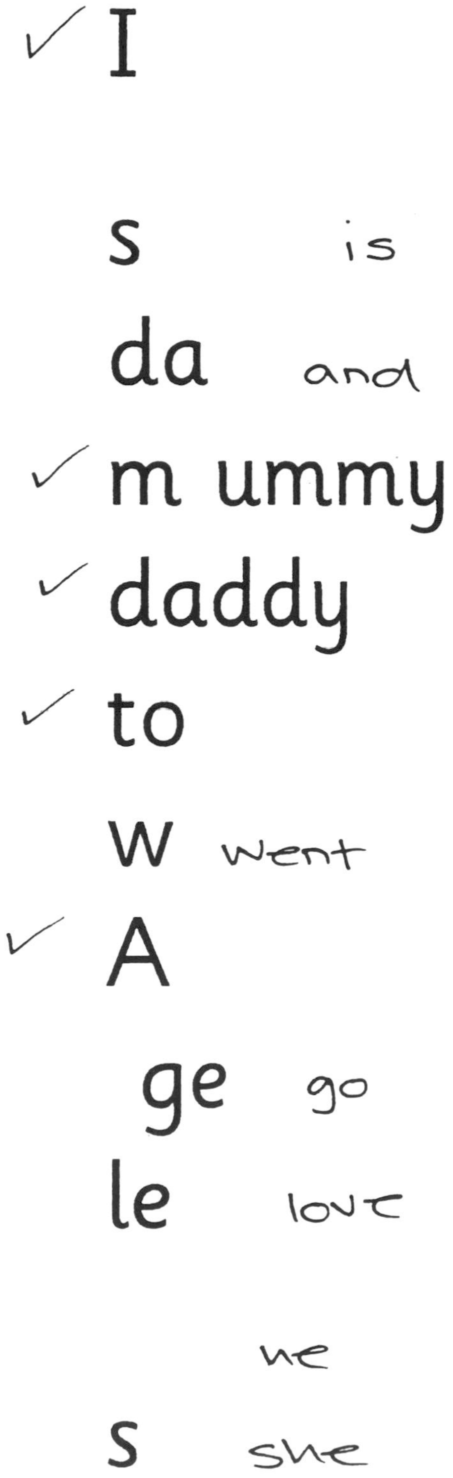

✓ I

s   is

da   and

✓ m ummy

✓ daddy

✓ to

W   went

✓ A

ge   go

le   love

           ne

s   she

Figure 20 Hannah's spelling challenge

home-educated by her mother, Hannah had a good idea of the grip required to hold a pencil, however she found it very hard to develop control. When the occupational therapist visited, she told us that Hannah would find her writing easier when she had some wrist support in the form of a glove. She was being fitted for one of these. She also suggested the use of slightly thicker pencils for Hannah that would also help her to grip more easily. Hannah's family provided these.

At the beginning of Year 1, Hannah had her own small pencil case containing felt-tip pens which were thicker than pencils, making them easier for her to hold. They were smooth flowing and allowed Hannah to form letters easily. She kept her pencil case in her drawer and knew to go and get it each time she needed to do some written work. There was a zip at the top of the pencil case and Hannah could not grasp the metal fastener as her 'pincer' grip was not fine enough. We found that by attaching a paper clip and elongating the fastener she could get enough purchase if another person held the pencil case firmly to allow her to open the zip herself. This epitomised Hannah's struggle towards independence. She was learning many new tasks but, at the same time, needed support to complete the most basic things.

Taking the top off her felt-tip pen was another huge achievement for Hannah. She could clutch the pen in her right hand and try to grip and pull the top off with her stronger left hand. Very often she did not have the strength to grip hard enough with her left hand and her hand slipped off the pen, leaving the top in place. Eventually she built up the strength for this manoeuvre, but again there was the dilemma. Do I spend the time practising this particular fine motor skill, or do I remove the top and let Hannah get on with handwriting practice?

Putting the top back on the pen was also very difficult for Hannah. Her eye–hand co-ordination was inhibited by an 'intention' tremor, which occurred whenever the top got near to the pen. If I steadied her hand as she brought the top closer, she could manage to position it correctly. She then placed the pen, top down, vertical to the work surface, and pushed down with her weight. This manoeuvre would snap the top into place and Hannah could do it unaided.

For handwriting practice Hannah needed the following aids:

- Glove
- Thick felt-tip pen
- Sloping desk top
- Foot stool in position
- Non-slip mat on the foot stool
- Her own chair with side panels attached
- Blu-Tack®[1] to stick the paper or book to the sloping desk.

Hannah then sat with other children at a table with me next to her. I would put the glove on her. As it was quite tight, it was difficult to do until I got used to it. Her sloping desktop arrived in the spring term of Year 2 (see figure 21) . Prior to that, we used a large lever arch file as a substitute which seemed to work well. It is worth mentioning here that when equipment arrives, it is important to have some training in its correct use. I did not realise that I had to position the sloping desktop with the lower end placed over the edge of the table. Until my error was pointed out, I had the whole thing on top of the table, which made it harder for Hannah to use.

---

[1] Blu-Tack® is a registered trademark of Bostik Ltd.

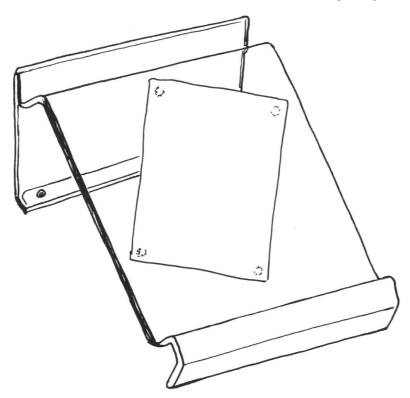

Figure 21 Hannah's sloping desk showing correct positioning of paper

It was very important to ensure that Hannah was well positioned before she began writing. She was asked to sit upright and back in her chair so that she was well supported. Her footstool, with its non-slip mat, was in position so that her feet were flat on it and the angle between her back and her thighbone was approximately 90 degrees. The occupational therapist and physiotherapists explained that the upright posture and 'centring' would increase Hannah's dexterity and pencil control.

The children in Year 1 had progressed in their writing from using unlined books of approximately A4 size, to smaller, lined exercise books. This was inappropriate for Hannah who was still working on the basic shape of letters. We were not worried about the size. She therefore continued to write on A4-size plain paper and would use up many sheets during each session. This was because paper was easier than a heavier book to stick down and keep still. If she did not have Blu-Tack® to hold her paper she found it imposs- ible to write as, with her rather sweeping movements, the paper would move away from her. As Hannah was left handed, it was important to have the paper positioned at a slant with the left-hand corner upper most. This enabled her to move on to the next letter more easily.

Hannah also held a large, cylindrical shape in her right hand whilst she did her writing. The occupational therapist explained that this would help Hannah 'centre' herself and allow her to concentrate on the fine motor skills that she was trying to perform with her left hand. We used, for this purpose, a thick white-board marker that we kept in her pencil case. Once Hannah knew that this formed part of the writing routine, she was far better at remembering to use it than I was.

Art

Art was an important part of the curriculum for Hannah. Her mother explained to us that Hannah did not like any activity that made her hands messy or wet. She had been described as 'tactile defensive' by the occupational therapist. Artwork, which often involved painting and gluing, was therefore quite a challenge for her. At first she would refuse to do it, or do it only until her hands became dirty and then stop. Gradually we introduced her to using a paintbrush and doing some sticking. Hannah willingly put on her art apron, with help, and enjoyed standing at the art table with the other children. The aim in these sessions was to get Hannah to choose a variety of colours and also to try to fill the whole page with her work. She was inclined to paint only the centre of the paper with one colour and go over and over on the same spot until the wetness of the paint would make a hole. We guided her hand to the other parts of the paper and encouraged her to use different paints. It was important to hold the paint pots steady as she inserted and removed her brush. Light yoghurt pots were used and these could easily tip over, spoiling her work and that of her peers.

Another objective for art was for Hannah to produce something recognisable. She knew where to put the elements of a face, for example, but she found it very hard to control a long paintbrush. She often needed help to keep the eyes, nose and mouth within the outline of any face she drew. This did not stop her obvious enjoyment, especially when every face she drew was Ardy, her favourite uncle!

Music

Music was a great love of Hannah's. Although she found it quite hard to sit through a long assembly without fidgeting, as soon as the music teacher started on the piano, Hannah was riveted and ready to join in with the singing. At first she just listened very intently to the other children singing, but as I became more comfortable with signing, Hannah turned to me to see what signs she could do for the words in time with the music. Although Makaton does not have signs for many of the words that were in the songs, we managed very well. Hannah could have a go at signing some of the words of every song that the school sang. It worked so well that gradually other children spontaneously joined in with the signing, looking around at the classroom assistants to learn for themselves. At first they found it hard to learn from Hannah, as her signs were often indistinct; but gradually, as they got used to her, they watched her in order to learn. It was also a game that Hannah played a lot with her friends in the playground – choosing which song to sing and signing it all together. For this reason it was a very important part of her curriculum.

Hannah was always keen to play an instrument in any class music lessons and it was important to give her one that she could manage with her level of motor skill. She was generally very co-operative and played her drum or shook her tambourine at the appropriate time, unlike some of the children in her class!

Science

Science was normally studied in the afternoons, when Hannah was sometimes a little tired. We made the lessons as practical as possible and usually shortened the session, which helped retain her interest, She knew that if she worked hard for 20 minutes she could then play a favourite computer game or go into the home corner. When the class were learning about plants I drew a plant on a piece of A3 paper and cut out the different parts. We then labelled the petals, the roots and the stem and she signed the different colours and coloured them in.

Figure 22 Learning about plants on the computer

Hannah enjoyed the practical experience of growing seeds and beans and would keep a simple diary of the changes that occurred.

'My World for Windows'© on the RM Window Box™ allowed her to explore plants, life cycles and the weather.

Humanities

Humanities were studied in modules and normally took place in the afternoon. We took a very practical approach. When we studied the Victorians we were doubtful that Hannah fully understood that we were talking about something that happened 100 years ago, but she enjoyed looking at and handling the artefacts that we borrowed from a local museum. Hannah was able to explore and play with Victorian toys and dolls with the other children.

In Science and Humanities she worked with different groups of children and benefited from their varied approaches. It was not considered a good idea for Hannah to work always with her closest friends. By working with different groups she could expand her social interaction and not be as reliant on her special friends.

These shared experiences all helped to integrate Hannah, making her very much part of the class.

Class assembly

Once a term, each class in the school held a 'class assembly' when all the children in that class performed for the rest of the school. The topic of the assembly was related to the children's work and they displayed items they had made and often performed a short play. Hannah was up there with the others. She delighted in performing in front of the whole school and the only difference between her and the others was that she had a crouching classroom assistant next to her, making sure she did not fall over as they all stood up! The classroom support also vocalised any of Hannah's signs so that we were sure that the message got across.

Standard Attainment Tests

During the summer term the government requires Standard Attainment Tests (SATs) to be taken by school children at the end of a Key Stage. The first of these tests are those at the end of Key Stage 1 and are in English (writing, reading and spelling) and Maths. Teachers assess the levels attained in Science. If it is inappropriate for a child to be exposed to these tests they can be disapplied (i.e. not entered for them). The Special Needs Co-ordinator, Hannah's class teachers and classroom support discussed SATs with Hannah's mother and it was decided that she should take them along with her peers.

For children with special needs there are extra guidelines provided in the booklet accompanying the tests. These help prevent such children from being disadvantaged. They are able to use the various aids, such as a computer, that they normally use in their classroom work, and they are given extra time for their particular communication difficulties. In Hannah's case this involved time for signing. Like the other children, Hannah was taken out of the class into a quiet room for her reading test. This was quite straightforward. She approached the set text with confidence and signed her way through. She attempted to answer all the questions. Spelling was carried out on the computer and Hannah attempted most of the words, often correctly putting the initial sound and sometimes the whole word. The writing SAT was difficult for Hannah. It was attempted but not pursued.

During Hannah's Mathematics SAT both classroom assistants were needed to support her due to the practical nature of the test. One assistant documented Hannah's response and the results, and the other communicated with her what was required and helped her with some of the motor function that was needed such as using scales. Hannah found this SAT very hard due to the sometimes abstract nature of the test and it was decided to discontinue half way through, when Hannah was experiencing obvious difficulty. It was also not easy to assess Hannah's level of scientific knowledge due to her limited ability to communicate the more abstract scientific signs.

Despite these challenges, Hannah attempted all the tests required of a Year 2 child. Even though she struggled with some aspects of them, she tackled each task with enthusiasm and vigour. It was this approach, above all others that characterised her day-to-day learning throughout her infant schooling.

Class teachers' views

Tricia Robinson and Sue Small, Hannah's class teachers in Years 1 and 2 had no previous experience of working with a child with such severe disabilities and requiring one-to-one full-time support. They were both apprehensive at the start:

> Our main concern initially was how were we going to communicate with Hannah. The training we had in Makaton as a whole school was invaluable. What we didn't realise at the time, not knowing Hannah, was how helpful she was going to be. She helped us teach her by being so receptive and yet so patient when we failed to understand her.
>
> Hannah's inclusion ran very smoothly. Her IEP, set out by her specialist teacher and then implemented by the classroom support, ensured that her presence didn't intrude on our day to day teaching. Hannah was simply another member of our class. She had to abide by the class rules and the other children accepted her as one of them. We told her off in the same way we told the other children off if she was doing something she shouldn't, i.e. talking on the carpet.
>
> Teaching Hannah was so very rewarding. She was full of fun and had such a good sense of humour. She was willing to be teased, except when she was tired. When we think of Hannah we smile. We were very lucky to be her teachers.
>
> Tricia Robinson and Sue Small, Class teachers

There was no doubt about it. Hannah worked very hard. Pressing one key on the computer keyboard, forming a letter by hand or picking up a domino took a large amount of physical effort. Despite this, she took an active part in every area of the curriculum. The work was differentiated so that it was at an appropriate level, but Hannah was immersed in the day to day learning that took place, just like her classmates.

Key points

- Be empathic to the fact that a child receiving one-to-one support is given an intense workload with no day dreaming allowed and may tire easily.
- Ensure the child feels safe and comfortable before embarking on academic skills.
- Allow the child the opportunity of working alone, with a partner, in a group and with their class teacher, as well as with their support assistant.
- Make sure children working in a group are compatible with one another.
- Gather all resources and materials at the beginning of each lesson.
- When making resources use concepts that are particularly relevant to the child, e.g. using pictures of ice-cream cones in counting.
- Ensure that when new equipment arrives you are shown how to use it. Do not assume that you can work it out on your own.
- Do not worry if the child appears not to be progressing. Most children reach a learning plateau or hit stumbling points. If the problem continues, seek professional advice.
- When you have a close one-to-one working relationship, be sensitive to the fact your anxieties can transfer onto the child.

- Break down lessons into manageable sessions, dependent upon the child's needs and the type of activity involved.
- Only take the child out of the classroom to work when absolutely necessary.
- When working in a group with the child, ensure the other children are not totally demanding of your attention.
- Repetitive work for the reinforcement of skills should be approached in different ways to avoid boredom.
- Make sure the child shares their work with the class teacher and class.
- Allow the child breathing space, particularly from the support assistant.
- Give them the opportunity to work independently.
- Ensure progress is monitored. Keep records up-to-date every day.
- Allow the child to follow the same daily timetable as the other children, even though lessons may be shorter.

13 Being different

Hannah started at Trafalgar Infant School because her parents wanted her to experience her education in a mainstream school, just like any other child. They did not want her to be separated in a special school or unit. At Trafalgar she wore the school uniform, followed the school rules, joined in all the class and school activities and experienced the same ups and downs at play time as any other child. She had friends whom she sometimes fell out with and developed her own preferences when it came to schoolwork.

But there was no getting away from it: Hannah was different. Being unable to speak or walk meant that she stood out from the other children. She was immediately noticeable in the playground because of her walking frame. She had a helper with her, or nearby, for most of the day which other children did not have; and there was this strange signing that seemed to accompany her wherever she went!

Hannah was physically different. She was a small child who was by far the shortest in her class. She was also the eldest by at least a year. At first children would ask a lot of questions. Is she really eight years old? What are those things in her ears for? Why does she need that metal thing with wheels? In response to some questions I would say, 'Ask Hannah'. She loved to use her fingers for counting and could hold up the correct number for her age. Sometimes the children needed a translation; with her lack of motor control, it wasn't always obvious how many fingers Hannah was holding up! I would explain about the hearing aids and the frame as it was rather beyond Hannah's signing to cope with those sorts of questions. Soon the children achieved a relaxed acceptance of Hannah and her differences.

One aspect of Hannah's life in the school that made her stand out was the fact that everyone knew her name. She would walk into the hall and all the dinner ladies would greet her with, 'Hello Hannah'. She was well known in the Local Education Authority (LEA) and visitors to the school from the LEA would say, 'You must be Hannah. I've heard a lot about you.' Children would tell their parents about this little girl in the school who used a frame to walk and had a special helper. Soon children, teachers, parents, helpers and support staff all knew her and would greet her by name.

This must have been quite hard for her brother, Ari. He was over a year younger than Hannah and yet was in the same year group as her, although never in the same class. He would sometimes be seen in terms of his relationship with the famous Hannah and a newcomer might greet him with 'Oh, are you Hannah's brother?' rather than 'What is your name?'. He coped with this well and was able to show his anger and irritation at times, just like any other brother. The difficulty was recognised by the school staff and Ari was singled out for some special jobs in the school. He would, on occasions, be asked to go to all the classes and tell the teachers of any changes to assembly time. He loved this extra attention and would proudly carry out his new responsibility. In this way he was 'special' too.

When it came to schoolwork Hannah did, as far as possible, just what her classmates were doing throughout the day. Her work was differentiated to suit her needs but she missed out on very little that was going on. She was in a colour group just like the others. This told her where to sit and where to put her reading folder. She would work at the table with the children with her classroom support sitting beside her. Hannah's computer, however, made her different. It was placed against a wall in the classroom and she often used it for her maths work and English. She also enjoyed games on her computer when it was 'free choice' time for the children. She moved to her computer when the need arose but it did not seem to disrupt the class or bother Hannah. In fact it was sometimes a useful break for her to move around a little after she had been concentrating hard on her work.

Because of Hannah's physical impairment, she needed intensive one-to-one support in the classes which involved a lot of physical activity such as physical education (PE) and

Figure 23 Hannah in a PE lesson supported by Liz Wise

swimming. PE lessons were amongst Hannah's favourite class activities. She went with the others to get her PE bag off the peg and brought it back to the classroom to change. However Hannah needed to sit down on her chair to take her clothes off. She would remove her glasses and hearing aids, toss them on the table and proceed to pull her top off over her head. It was interesting that a child who was watching Hannah at this time suddenly said, 'Haven't you got funny eyes!' This was the first time that Hannah's facial features had been openly acknowledged by a child who was seeing her without glasses. My response was: 'Hannah has Downs syndrome and her eyes are a little different. It is also that people look different when we suddenly see them without their glasses on.'

The classroom assistant's job was to rescue the glasses and hearing aids and help Hannah on with her PE shirt. She could then stand up, but needed assistance pulling down her skirt and getting her legs into her shorts. She did not change her shoes but continued to wear her trainers. She then needed help to put her hearing aids back in. She could manage her glasses. We debated whether to spend time waiting while Hannah tried to change independently. This could have taken up a large amount of the PE lesson and Hannah would have missed the warm-up and instructions. We therefore decided to help her on these occasions and get her out to the hall or the playground as quickly as possible.

Hannah joined in with the other children for the PE lesson with some adaptations. She tried throwing and catching, using a beanbag instead of a ball. She balanced, climbed and even ran with a lot of support from her helper! No one embarked on a PE lesson using the apparatus with as much enthusiasm as Hannah. She tackled it fearlessly and with gusto, requiring her teacher and classroom support to be extra vigilant. This resulted in an inevitable tiredness for Hannah. There was an occasion in an early PE lesson when Hannah bit her helper. The teacher had been asking her to do too much and this was her only way of forcibly saying, 'I can't. I'm too tired.' After this incident, if she seemed to be flagging, we would sit out and have a rest while the other children carried on. She never had to bite again. We had all learned to listen more closely to her signals. Hannah never asked to go back to the classroom on these occasions. She was always very happy to stay and watch her friends.

Trafalgar Infant School felt that swimming was an important part of the curriculum and all the children in Year 2 had the opportunity to attend swimming lessons at the local pool. These were organised in two six-weekly sessions for a class at a time. The children loved the 'outing' in the coach and the different experience of the swimming baths. Hannah was no exception. She had to be carried to the coach, as it was too far to walk, but she loved getting on the bus, sitting with her friends and signing which songs she wanted to sing during the journey!

Hannah launched herself into the swimming itself (see figure 24). She had no fear and had no concerns about taking her feet off the bottom. The only problem was that, without support, she sank! I therefore stayed close to her, supporting her in her various swimming exercises. She was even keen to go underwater. This I found rather worrying as Hannah did not close her mouth at these times and I had visions of her choking and getting very upset. This didn't happen and I can only assume she somehow held the water in her mouth, preventing it entering her lungs.

During play time in the winter months, we noticed that Hannah's fingers went very blue and that she seemed to feel the cold more than other children do. It was decided, on these cold days, to keep her in the warm classroom for most of her breaks. She could always choose which friends to have with her to play. They were always very keen and would jump at the chance of being inside, away from the cold!

Figure 24 Hannah swimming with Chris Glass

In Year 1, Hannah found the full day quite difficult to cope with at first. She became very tired in the afternoons and it was decided to give her a rest whilst the others had afternoon play. We went to the kitchen (Hannah making her own way with her frame) where she had a drink of water and a quiet chat with her helper. She loved this time, especially as this was where children came with any knocks or grazes. Hannah could therefore do a great show of sympathising with them and enjoy seeing someone else at the receiving end of medical care!

Whole school activities also sometimes required adaptation in order for Hannah to be included. Watching Hannah participate in Sports Day each year was a very humbling experience. She was game for every activity being offered: egg and spoon races, dressing-up races, walking with a beanbag on your head. Most of these activities were team based and there was an element of competition. It was therefore quite important that the team Hannah was in did not feel disadvantaged. This meant that the classroom assistants had to work very hard on the day! We were both there to help Hannah and stood either side of her and whisked her along – her feet hardly touching the ground. We improvised and held the egg on the spoon and the beanbag on her head while we raced along. No one seemed to mind these minor alterations to the rules.

Another whole school activity that took place at the end of the Christmas term was 'Albert the Clown'. He was an entertainer who greatly amused the children with his singing, banjo playing and acrobatics. In Year 1 Hannah looked wide-eyed at the packed, noisy hall and Albert with his strange costume. At the first roar of laughter from the children, she began to make a loud howling noise and was obviously very distressed. We immediately left the hall and went to the peace of the classroom, where she stayed for the duration of his act. She could not be persuaded to go back in. By the time Hannah reached Year 2 she, like all the others, seemed to eagerly anticipate his arrival. Her confidence had grown and she was more able to tolerate noise and expose herself to new experiences. She was able to stay in the hall throughout Albert's act, despite all the screaming and cheering from the other children. She even volunteered for some of the acrobatic stunts but, perhaps thankfully for us, was not chosen!

One area of difference that could have caused a problem was the amount of money and resources being spent on Hannah. At first some parents expressed concern that so much could be invested in only one child. There were many children in the school who could benefit from one-to-one support for part of the school day, yet they were getting nothing. These feelings, however, were very short lived. The parents very quickly realised that far from getting nothing, their children were learning an enormous amount from having a little girl like Hannah in their midst. This was due in no small part to Hannah's sunny personality. She was warm and caring with a great sense of fun. The people she met could not help being captivated by her. There was no sense of pity. Instead the children maintained a relaxed acceptance of her difference and learnt patience, tolerance, respect and a rich and varied signing vocabulary.

Hannah's parents never interfered with her school life. They had confidence that the teachers and support staff would meet Hannah's learning needs and the children would sort out the social side. The only time I have heard them comment on the way Hannah was treated was in regard to the class photograph. She experienced one each summer term at the school. In every one of the three photos Hannah was at the side of the group with her classroom assistant standing beside her. Why had we never thought to put her in the middle with her friends? This seemed to symbolise the stage the school had got to in including Hannah. We were trying hard but despite this we could at times still unconsciously keep her on the edge of things. It was easier to have her at the side as she would be the last out into the playground for the photo. To put her in between two children would mean moving her classmates. In retrospect it would have been worth the effort. Hannah would be seen sitting amongst her friends with her helper on the sidelines.

We have seen that Hannah's difference did not cause any real difficulties in the day-to-day life of the school. She worked alongside her classmates, attended assembly, had lunch, enjoyed PE (with a little help!) and got told off just like the others. But there was one thing her difference did. It opened the school up and enabled the children, parents and staff to develop a fuller understanding of what difference means. Children with special educational needs have the same feelings as those children without special educational needs; they have the same rights to be educated and to have their independence fostered; they need the same firm boundaries and a caring, supportive environment in which to learn; they are individuals with their own unique sense of self. Through Hannah the whole school had learned a powerful lesson. She had paved the way for other children with very particular special educational needs who, like her, stood out as 'different'. Perhaps in future they will be seen not in terms of their disability, but as children just like the others.

Key points

- Be sensitive to the feelings of siblings of children with special needs in the same school. Give them a job to do to make them feel special too.
- Respond to children's questions about difference openly and honestly.
- If the child needs to stay in at play time, they need a friend to be with them Make up a list of friends and work through it so that it is not the same child each day.
- Balance the promotion of independence with the need for the child to experience an aspect of the curriculum, e.g. do not always spend half the PE lesson changing.
- If there is a group situation when you think the child may become upset, position yourself so that you can make a quick and easy exit with them.
- Be aware in group photographs of where you are positioning the child.
- Be sensitive to the concerns of parents of other children regarding the amount of resources dedicated to one child.
- Be prepared to put in extra effort so that a child is included in all school activities.

14 Moving on

Hannah had spent two years in Trafalgar Infant School. It was the summer term of Year 2 and her friends were just getting ready for their transition to the attached junior school. The transition from infant to junior, and junior to senior school, is a worrying time for all parents, but particularly for those who have children with special needs. Will the new school accept them? Will they still get the same level of support? Could the physical environment pose new problems? Will the Authority suggest a special school because 'the gap is getting wider' between the child and her peers?

When Hannah's teachers, classroom assistants and parents got together with the Authority for the annual review of her statement, there was an easy atmosphere. The various reports were presented and there seemed to be only positive outcomes for Hannah's time at school. The Special Educational Needs Co-ordinator (SENCO) from the junior school had some very pertinent questions regarding Hannah's reading and conceptual understanding. What would happen as books became more abstract, and the lessons with the other children required a higher cognitive level? She was understandably concerned that Hannah, who had found it so easy to fit in to the infant school, would become frustrated and feel pressurised when she found herself unable to do the same work as her peers. The educational psychologist also expressed concern that Hannah had no contact with children like herself. She suggested Hannah should spend some time, each week or so, with children in the local special school. She would then experience children who had the same sort of difficulties as she did. Hannah's parents, however, did not want this. They felt it would be of no benefit as Hannah mixed with such children outside school. To remove her from her class and transport her to another location would only disrupt her school day and interrupt her learning.

The review ended with a strongly positive feeling regarding Hannah's progress in mainstream school. Of course there would be new challenges but the over-riding feeling at the meeting was that she would be going on to the junior school with her friends.

There followed a series of visits to the school for Hannah and the other children. They were given their new classes and Hannah was thrilled to be with quite a few good friends. The mother of one of the boys in Hannah's class had made a request for him to stay in the same class as Hannah. She felt he had benefited enormously from being with her by becoming more sensitive and aware. He was not even a particular friend.

The new classroom was quite cramped and was to be re-organised to accommodate Hannah's computer. The only other problem seemed to be the stairs down to the school toilets. A rail would have to be fitted for Hannah and her frame would have to be carried up and down for her. This meant a loss of independence in this area, but it seemed a small price to pay for the excitement and experience of another new school.

Hannah was now orientated to her junior school. We had introduced her to her new SEN classroom supports and class teacher and met separately with them to discuss Hannah's needs. The following 'Welcome to Hannah' notes were given to them as an easy guide to Hannah's day-to-day management.

WELCOME TO HANNAH
Chris Glass and Liz Wise
22 June, 1998

These notes are to introduce you to Hannah, to act as a guide to what to expect and to be reassuring.

Staff communication

As the basis for Hannah's successful inclusion, communication between all members of staff involved is of paramount importance.

We (classroom support) have a half-hour meeting on a Monday morning at 8.30. We use this time to share concerns and points of interest from the previous week and to establish Hannah's timetable for the next week. We then may take any relevant points to the class teacher and/or SENCO.

At the end of each morning and afternoon session, we complete Hannah's timetable (see attached) and fill in relevant notes for her IEPs in her IEP recording book. Hannah keeps a home/school diary and we use this for information that should be going home.

We prepare a progress report before parent/teacher meetings as a guide for the class teachers.

Hannah's day-to-day management

Hannah's day is based around developing her independence. She is brought into the class and then walks to the carpet with the aid of her friends. We put her hearing aids in at this point, having checked the batteries are working. (Hannah is rather reluctant to wear two, but can usually be persuaded.)

We always greet Hannah with signing 'Good morning' and 'How are you?' The class teacher when she takes the register signs 'Good morning' and looks for Hannah's response. At this point Hannah listens to what the day's activities are to be with the other children, and then depending on the appropriateness of the work Hannah stays with the class or we take her to work on her individual IEP programme.

For play times, assembly, singing, library, lunch time and class activities outside the classroom Hannah is accompanied by two other children who support her in walking and the basic needs. However, we are always in the background.

Hannah moves around the classroom using the furniture as a support and can manage to walk small distances on her own. It is important to be near her when she walks without support as she can overbalance or trip up quite easily and may need to be caught. We have talked with Mrs Levy, and have minuted the fact that, as Hannah's independence grows, there is a risk of her falling.

Hannah is left to her own devices in the playground and is usually soon joined by two or three friends. Again, we are in the background and probably spend more time with other children than with Hannah. Using her frame, she lines up with the rest of the class.

The same follows for lunchtime, with an adult in the background checking on Hannah every few minutes in case she has a choking episode with her food (this has not happened for several months).

Hannah usually goes to the toilet once a day. She can go on her own with her frame, enter the toilet and close the door. She needs her foot stool which we take into the toilet for her. Holding a hand on the wall she can pull her knickers down if her dress/skirt is held up. She can climb onto the toilet, wipe herself and climb off, pull up her pants and pull the flush, wash and dry her hands and go back to class. (If she opens her bowels she needs her bottom wiped).

At the end of the day we spend ten minutes working on Hannah's symbols (usually taken out of play time). Example attached. This allows Hannah to share with her family what she has done during the day and is another form of communication for Hannah.

Classroom special aids

- Computer – Hannah needs access to this at all times
- Chair – Hannah uses this for all activities
- Footstool – Hannah uses this whilst working in the chair
- Sloping Desk Top – Hannah uses this for writing and drawing activities
- Support glove – Hannah wears this for all fine motor skills
- Blu-Tack® – for positioning paper at an angle onto the desktop
- Large felt-tip pens
- Large exercise books.

Individual Education Plan

Hannah's IEP is evaluated and updated with the special needs consultant once a term. The current programme is in her file.

Hannah's gross motor skills and speech programme are both designed by the relevant therapists. We are responsible for carrying out her physio programme once a week for twenty minutes and her speech programme twice a week for twenty minutes.

Helpful hints

- You may find Hannah's signing incomprehensible at first but you will get used to it. Hannah is very patient and understanding if her signing is not understood.
- Hannah has a great sense of humour and will tell you when she is being cheeky by pinching her cheek.

- Hannah can be reluctant sometimes to respond to instruction but with encouragement and firmness will finally get there.
- Hannah has a younger brother, Ari in the same year. People should be aware that Hannah receives a great deal of attention and be sensitive of her brother's needs – moving into the junior school is a big move for Ari too.
- Hannah rarely cries but when she does she howls and it can sound alarming. We do not encourage Hannah to hug and cuddle during a normal day but when she is really upset a cuddle works a treat.
- Hannah will quite often be found chewing around her nails and we discourage this.
- Hannah quite often complains of sore knees; Mrs Levy is aware of this and her new leg supports should help.

In conclusion, working with Hannah is a unique experience. Despite her many disabilities, Hannah remains brave, cheerful and hardworking. We have gained a lot from working with Hannah over the past two years and so have the children and staff in the school. Working with Hannah can be tiring but rewarding. If you have any concerns, please phone us at home or at school.
GOOD LUCK!

Chris and Liz

Hannah only had a few days left in the infant school. As her one-to-one supporters for over two years, we decided we wanted to buy her a joint present. We chose a large, cuddly teddy bear. Hannah loved to cuddle and care for such toys. We gave it to her on the last day of term in the privacy of one of the small rooms. It was a very emotional time for us. We tried to explain to Hannah what a privilege it had been to work with her and how we would miss her. We would hear how she was getting on in the junior school and we were sure she would be just fine.

As we read out our card to Hannah, with our individual comments, both of us found our voices breaking. She could not speak or walk; she had to work hard to carry out the simplest of tasks; she had to try and make friends with the burden of an adult constantly close by; but she managed all of these things. She was her own person. She was funny, loyal, sensitive and caring. She was naughty, cheeky, determined, brave and hard working. She had shown all those who had doubts that a child with severe disability can be educated in a mainstream school; and not only that. She had had a positive impact on the whole culture of the school. She had changed people's attitudes and taught the other children and adults so much about disability and difference.

She was indeed special.

Afterword
A note from Hannah's parents

It was a momentous day for us all when Hannah entered mainstream education. We knew that the staff had concerns and we had our moments of anxiety, but Hannah appeared unaffected. On that first day she walked into the classroom and sat on the carpet with all the other children. She looked great in her school uniform, proudly displaying her Trafalgar emblem. Hannah was a schoolgirl at last; we could now step back, knowing that she was receiving an education that was not totally our responsibility. We felt an enormous satisfaction at having got to this stage.

During her time at the school, she progressed in all areas of her development. This was due to the help and encouragement she received from those in her class – the support workers, her teachers and the children. School helpers, parents and, of course, other children around the school, were also of immense importance. Everyone treated Hannah with respect and this reinforced our belief that Hannah's rightful place was at Trafalgar.

Hannah had some wonderful experiences in the Infants. She was always eager to get to school to see her friends and teachers. Children came up to greet her in the playground saying and signing, 'Hello Hannah!' Everyone in the school was learning some Makaton and many of the children were keen to develop this skill. Other parents were proud of their children's signing ability and said as much to us. When we attended school assemblies we noticed that Hannah's schoolmates, both boys and girls, would hold her hand to support her as they walked into assembly. Sometimes she'd sneak in a quick chat with her neighbour as she waited for assembly to begin, and there would be some silent (or not so silent!) signing conversation going on. It was a very moving experience for us to see children throughout the assembly hall attempting to sign the songs along with Hannah. The whole school was making an effort to include her and children were enjoying themselves at the same time.

At school Hannah had the chance to form friendships in her own right. Going out to tea or to birthday parties became a regular event. Hannah was always keen to return the favour and entertain her friends, and her birthday parties were memorable events. She also attended Brownies with her friends from school and we took turns in driving the girls back and forth.

When the time had come for her class to move from the infant school to the junior school we had a strong belief that Hannah's character, attitude and hard endeavour would be justifications for continuing her in mainstream education. Many of her classmates' parents expected Hannah to move up with their children and we are delighted that this has turned out to be the case.

Since Hannah's first day at Trafalgar we have been happy to take a step back from being solely responsible for her schooling. We have always had a positive attitude towards

Hannah and what she is capable of achieving. It has been our good fortune that Hannah's teachers and helpers shared in this. The importance of such a positive approach cannot be overstated. By combining it with Hannah's unique character she has been able to show what she can offer. She has given us all a feeling of quiet satisfaction that we hope will continue for many years to come.

Alayne and Michael Levy

Appendix 1

Support Assistant

30 hours - term time only

Salary £10,667.08 (includes Outer London Allowance and Special Schools Allowance)

A support assistant is required for September 1996, to support a child with a high level of learning difficulty in a mainstream infant school.

The post will be for one year in the first instance but with a possibility of being renewed annually.

For application form, further details (S.A.E. please), and to arrange a visit please contact the Headteacher Mrs L Thompson.

The closing date for applications is 21st June 1996. Interviews will be at the school on July 3rd.

Appendix 2

Support Assistant – Job Description (30 hrs term time only)
Job shares are welcomed.

Responsible to: Head teacher, Trafalgar Infant School

Main responsibilities

The essential purpose is to enable the child to gain maximum access to the mainstream school curriculum and to support social integration with peers. There will be a need to maintain a balance between supporting when help is needed and allowing the child to develop maximum independence.

It is the teacher(s) who has primary responsibility for the child's learning. The support assistant is there to help the teacher(s) and the child, working under the teacher's direction, with additional support and advice from specialist advisory teachers and other professionals.

Main duties

These may include:

- Supervising the practice of skills
- Assisting the child when there are mobility problems
- Adapting teaching materials to make them accessible when necessary
- Providing practical help, ensuring the child's safety in activities such as PE, school outings, etc.
- Reinforcing the child's learning using specialised equipment
- Giving support when necessary with eating, dressing, washing and using the toilet
- Contributing to record keeping, reports and review meetings.

In addition, the support assistant may be called upon by the teacher to work with other children or do tasks which could be reasonably expected of her and which would enhance the inclusive nature of this child's education.

Person specification – support assistant

- Must be supportive of inclusive education
- Must have flexible attitude and be able to work co-operatively with colleagues

- Must be able to follow direction
- Must be willing to use, or learn how to use, specialist equipment
- Must be able to use Makaton signing or be prepared to train in its use
- Must have had some previous, relevant experience of working with children or young people in a paid or voluntary capacity
- Must have, or be prepared to train for, a first aid qualification.

Additional information

The post is for one year in the first instance with a possibility of renewal annually. If the child is absent, the support assistant will be expected to work in any part of the school on any duties that can reasonably be expected by the teacher.

Appendix 3

Individual Education Plan – Hannah Levy

An overview

Independence

- General approach
- Use of toilet
- Independent working
- Eating
- Drinking.

Gross motor skills

- High kneeling
- Half-kneeling
- Walking with sticks.

Speech programme

- Sensory stimulation and facial awareness
- Lip exercises
- Phonic sounds b, m. and p.

English

- Use multiple signs to express self
- Record a recent event
- Spelling.

Maths

- Counting 6–10
- Make sets of 1–5 objects.

Fine motor skills

- Drawing/writing.

Art

- Produce simple recognisable objects in a picture
- Cover the whole area of paper.

Computer

- Copy-type independently.

Breakdown of objectives

Independence

General approach

Encourage total independence whenever possible. This can be done in various situations, and can be added to as physical and independence skills develop, i.e. adult sits in the classroom during assembly, Year singing etc. and for sessions where other staff are not normally in attendance. A named fellow pupil can be used to call for assistance if necessary.

During play times the adult can withdraw and observe from a distance, only interacting if the need arises.

Use of toilet

1   Remove necessary clothing in order to use the toilet
2   Use paper independently
3   Replace clothing.
    • Encourage Hannah to tuck her dress under her chin to keep it out of the way
    • Encourage her to use one hand to hold the toilet roll steady, the other to tear the paper.

Independent working

1   Work independently of any adult help, using familiar worksheets.

Eating

1   Place food in the side of the mouth to aid chewing
2   Move food around the mouth with the tongue rather than the fingers
3   Finish a mouthful before putting more food in.

Drinking

1   Sit with elbows on the table, holding the cup with both hands.

Gross motor skills

High kneeling

1   Balancing
2   Reaching games
3   Throwing and catching beanbag
4   Turning body to look behind.

Half kneeling

1   Try alternate leg up (holding hands if necessary)
2   Balance.

Walking with sticks

Walk placing opposite foot forward to stick i.e. right foot/left stick. (Put like-coloured stickers on foot/stick that move together.)

Speech programme

Sensory stimulation and facial awareness

1   Use a variety of materials and brushes to develop facial sensory awareness, using short, quick tapping movements around cheek, mouth and chin areas
2   *Only stimulate one side of the face at a time.* Ask Hannah to indicate on a drawn face where she can feel it on her own.

Equipment: a variety of brushes and materials of different textures.

Lip exercises

1   Activities to encourage lip rounding.
    • Using a mirror encourage Hannah to copy an 'o' shape
    • Push lips forward into a kissing position
    • Apply lipstick and make round prints on paper
    • Blow whistles, party blowers etc. that have round mouthpieces. Hold with lips not teeth

- Blow out cake candles with rounded lips.
- Blow out cake candles through a straw or plastic tubing. Hold with lips not teeth
- Play blow football using straws and ping-pong balls, cotton wool or tissue paper.

2   Activities to encourage putting lips together.
- Use lips to pick up sweets, raisins, etc.
- Apply lipstick and make prints of lips together on paper.

3   Activities to encourage lip spreading.
- Lip printing to make a smile print.

4   Activities to encourage changes in lip space.
- Without speech sounds, change from round to spread shape, e.g. pretend to be a fish then a clown
- Make lip prints of different shapes.

Equipment: Mirror, lipstick, instruments with round mouth pieces, candles, straws, tubing, tissue paper, cotton wool, bubbles.

Phonic sounds b, m and p

1   Play lotto games using Language Master. Encourage Hannah to make sounds during the game
2   Blow out candles with a 'p' sound.

Equipment: Lotto pack, Language Master.

English

Use multiple signs to express self

1   Encourage Hannah to answer questions with more than one sign, e.g. 'Where are you going?' 'I'm going to play'
2   Describe picture using simple sentences
3   Re-tell simple familiar story (use favourite books).

Record a recent event

Hannah to learn to create a written record of a recent event. An adult will write down Hannah's signed words for her to copy either on the computer, or by hand. This activity must be carried out immediately after the event whilst it is still fresh in her mind.

Spelling

Hannah to work on Year 1 spelling list using finger spelling, writing and the computer.

Maths

Counting 6–10

1   Count objects 6–10 in a straight line, pointing to each object in turn. Indicate final number on a number line and by showing correct number of fingers
2   Count out objects by placing them under a number line 6–10
3   Count moveable objects, i.e. move each object as it is counted. Use cue card to reinforce memorising number.

Make sets of 1–5 objects

1   Place objects on cards numbered 1–5
2   Give adult 1–5 objects when asked. Use cue card to reinforce memorising number.

Fine motor skills

Drawing/writing

1   Keep a drawn line within a given boundary, to include letter and number formation. Reduce width of boundary lines as skill develops
2   Tracing over dotted numbers/letters to establish starting/finishing points and direction.

Resources: Worksheets, thick pencils.

Art

Produce simple recognisable objects in a picture

1   Observe simple objects or pictures of objects
2   Copy them with particular emphasis on shape and colour.

Cover the whole area of paper

1   Use the whole area of paper
2   Use a number of different colours.

Computer

Copy-type independently

1   Copy-type simple single words
2   Copy-type short sentences
3   Copy-type a short sentence, including punctuation.

Appendix 4

English			
Date	Activity	Comments	☺

Appendix 5

Daily Record	
Date	Comments

Appendix 6

Hannah Levy
Date of Birth: 4th August 1989

ANNUAL REVIEW OF STATEMENT
Wednesday, 6 May 1998

Report prepared by: *Christine Glass and Liz Wise*
Classroom Support
Trafalgar Infant School

Introduction

Hannah completed Year 1 in Yellow Room following her annual review in June 1997. During the academic year 96/97 Hannah was supported by Helena Chambers (0.5 Support Teacher) and Christine Glass and Liz Wise (Classroom support job share).

In September 1997 Hannah commenced Year 2 in Yellow Room. She continued to be supported by Christine Glass and Liz Wise with Helena Chambers acting in a consultancy role, visiting Hannah once a term and re-setting her objectives for her Individual Educational Plan. This approach has worked well with Christine and Liz working alongside Yellow Room's class teachers Tricia Robinson and Sue Small and Sally Kralj, SENCO.

Hannah had no difficulty settling back into school after the summer break. She knew Yellow Room, her teachers and support staff well and some of her classmates from Year 1 were also in her Year 2 class.

One of our main objectives this year has been to develop and establish Hannah's independence.

Overview

In all areas of Hannah's IEPs she has made varying degrees of progress as this report will show.

One of the most important aspects this year is the development of Hannah's independence. Hannah goes into Assembly and singing in the Hall on her own where her attention can be kept for 30 minutes. She goes to the Library on her own to find a book and then will return to Yellow Room.

Hannah's confidence and ability to cope with different situations has grown. An example of this was when Albert the Clown came to visit. The previous year we had to take her from the Hall because she was frightened by the noise and excitement. However Christmas 1997 was very different with Hannah laughing and giggling the whole way through Albert the Clown, and even wanting to go up and meet him after the show. Albert himself commented on the change.

The arrival of the computer in the 1997 Autumn term has been a tremendous asset. Not only has it been able to develop Hannah's independent working, many of the programmes have enhanced her day to day learning.

During this year Hannah has made some very special new friendships in the class and remains popular with her peers – each and every child in the class willingly and eagerly takes on the role of supporting Hannah with a variety of activities.

Hannah enjoys playtime and always has plenty of friends to play with, from all year groups. Occasionally a friend will say to Hannah they want to play with someone else and Hannah shrugs her shoulders and accepts this without a fuss.

Hannah has enjoyed several school trips, venturing into different environments with delight. A note should be made here that Hannah is getting heavier and from time to time needs to be lifted and training should be given to Hannah's supporters in correct lifting techniques.

Hannah has numerous invitations out to tea and to birthday parties, and even though she is so popular she is not 'fussed' over.

She is just one of the children in Yellow Room.

Mobility

This is an area which has shown great improvement during the last year. Hannah has had no leg supports in Year 2 as she is awaiting a new fitting. Despite this, she can still get up from sitting on the floor to a standing position. She also appears more sure and more stable when standing on her own, which she can do for 20 seconds or so before becoming tired. She can stand unaided when carrying a heavy lunch box or bag. Her walking is also more stable and upright. She can walk the length of the hall, some 20 yards, with about three stops just to balance herself on a piece of furniture or a hand.

Hannah uses her new frame which arrived in September 1997. She walks to lunch using it, the library, the toilet and out to play. For moving around the classroom she uses furniture or an adult's hand. She is stopped from crawling.

Gross motor skills

Hannah continues with her physiotherapy at school for 15 minutes each week. She does it with another child from Yellow Room. Hannah can now kneel up on her own and walk forward on her knees for three to five feet unaided. She needs support when walking backwards on her knees but she remains much more upright and balanced than before.

Her throwing is improving and she can aim and propel a beanbag appropriately, although some times rather fast!

Going to the toilet

Hannah can now enter the toilet, close the door, climb up on the toilet with the aid of a wall handle and foot stool, tear off paper and attempt to wipe herself, climb back down and flush the toilet. In the colder months, when wearing tights, she can pull down her tights and pants with copious verbal encouragement! When only wearing pants she could probably pull them down and up unaided and therefore could be left to go to the toilet in private.

She washes her hands unaided.

Lunch time

Hannah continues to have a packed lunch. She always has classmates who want to sit next to her. She walks into lunch using her frame with her lunch box hanging from it. Space can be very constricted and at times her frame needs to be lifted over obstructions as she walks through.

Once seated Hannah eats her lunch independently apart from help to start peeling her banana. Up to now she has had help to open her lunch box, but it was noted when left alone with it during play time the other day she opened it herself!

Hannah has not had any problems with choking in Year 2 and so her helper can leave her for long periods over lunch time, merely keeping an eye on her every few minutes from the classroom.

Hannah enjoys lunch time and has made friends with the SMSA's and cooks who know her well and always chat to her.

Fine motor skills

Hannah has improved greatly in this area since having her glove and sloping work surface and being 'centred' in her sitting position whilst gripping an object in her right hand.

She enjoys writing and at present is following letters previously written out with a dotted line. These are slowly getting smaller as Hannah gains more control. Hannah seems to enjoy this activity and can concentrate well whilst doing it. She can also form some letters on her own.

Communication

It can be said without doubt that communication for Hannah can be tremendously difficult, but she works hard to make herself understood. She picks up new signs with ease and she has increased her signing vocabulary greatly. She has been introduced to a great many signs that cover the vocabulary that is relevant to the National Curriculum. Her signing is sometimes difficult to understand because of her poor co-ordination, but she does not appear to become frustrated when we cannot understand. She now uses a sign for 'I've had enough' when she wants to finish a task or is perhaps feeling cross.

She has been introduced to 'symbols' as a means of communication – using pictures with the written word and she has picked up the system very readily. She uses the system primarily to be able to communicate at home what she has done during the school day. (See Appendix 1). She is able to independently change the month and day and find the relevant symbols for what she has done during the day, with only minimal prompting.

Hannah is sensitive to other children's feelings and will empathise and be tremendously caring when someone is sad or upset. Equally she takes great pleasure in a child's happiness and will be the first child in the class to start laughing at a joke.

Speech work

We have reduced the number of 'formal' speech sessions from four to one or two a week. However she is actively encouraged to vocalise during all times of the day. In our formal speech session we use a mirror for Hannah to see herself opening and closing her mouth, hiding and poking out her tongue and making different shapes with her mouth. We use soft and rough items to encourage facial awareness. Hannah loves wearing a bright pink lipstick to then make a print with her mouth on a piece of paper to show the different shapes she can make!

Computer

The computer which arrived for Hannah during the Autumn term has been a tremendous asset, especially as it enables her to work independently. She is able to access the computer independently and find the right programme and shows great skill in controlling the rollerball. Hannah uses the computer for news writing, spelling challenges and maths work. When she is given 'choosing time' she will often elect to go to the computer to find a game.

Maths

For the last four months we have implemented an intensive maths programme for Hannah, spending 10 minutes each day on numberwork. She can sequence up to 20 and can find quickly any given number. She can competently make sets of objects up to 5 and just recently is mastering one to one correspondence of objects up to 10. Hannah uses 'Numberpics' on the computer for much of her numberwork. This programme actually records her answers which allows her to work independently, while also allowing us to follow her progress.

English

Hannah is building up her Year 1 CAT spellings, and understands about capital letters and full stops. She is able to sequence cut up words to form a sentence. When given a choice of 'News' topics she can choose the one that she would like to write about and with help put this into writing on the computer. Hannah finds comprehension hard, but by using a very simplified text and pictures to aid her understanding, she is making progress.

Summary

Hannah's bright sunny nature has made her a pleasure to work with and her sense of humour has lightened the load!

When considering Hannah's special needs it is quite remarkable how smoothly her time in school has progressed. She is rarely upset or demanding and remains co-operative and responsive to her supporters.

It has been enlightening to work with Hannah and she has given much to her peers and staff at Trafalgar Infant School.

Appendix 7

Appendix 8

Big Sister Rosie	
Where is Rosie?	
Where is Rosies' mum?	
Where is Rosies' dad?	
Where is Rosies' grandad?	
Where is the baby?	

Yellow Squares
Character recognition
Identify each character by pointing

Page no.	Understanding of text	
2	Who is having a baby?	Rosies' mum (sign)
3	Who painted the baby's room?	Rosies' dad (sign)
4	What did mum and Rosie paint?	Cot/bed (sign)
5	What did grandad do?	a) Painted a cot b) Washed pram c) Made a mobile
6	What did Rosie make for the baby?	Mobile (select from list)
7	Did Rosie paint a boy or a girl?	Girl (sign)
8	What did Rosie want to call the baby?	Daisy (sign D)
9	Where did mum go?	Hospital (sign)
	Why did she go to hospital?	To have a baby (sign)
10	Did the baby have any hair?	No (sign)
	Did the baby have any teeth?	No (sign)
	Was the baby a boy or a girl?	Boy (sign)
11	What did Rosie say when she saw the baby?	a) I wanted a baby boy b) I wanted a baby girl
12/13	What did the baby do when he came home?	Cried (sign)

Glossary

(AFO) ankle foot orthosis   A leg support for the ankle which helps with walking.

annual review   An annual review of the statement involving all agencies involved with the child.

aromatherapy massage   A massage using aromatherapy oils.

brushing   A technique used to heighten/tackle sensory awareness.

CENMAC   Centre for Micro-Assisted Communication.

clinical psychologist   A psychologist who applies psychological principles to the diagnosis and treatment of emotional and behavioural problems in children and adults.

cognitive skills   The ability to think and understand.

cranial osteopathy   Manipulation and massage of the small bones of the skull to assist with harmonising the body.

differentiation   Adapting the curriculum and environment to meet the child's needs.

Down's syndrome   A chromosomal abnormality first described in 1866 by John Langdon Down, a physician, in England.

echocardiogram   A medical procedure using sound waves to obtain an outline of the heart, allowing any abnormalities to be detected easily.

educational psychologist   A psychologist who applies psychological principals to tackle problems and difficulties of children and young people in an educational setting.

fine motor skills   Co-ordinated movements involving the small joints, e.g. handwriting.

gross motor skills   Co-ordinated movement of the arms and legs, e.g. walking, kicking.

Individual Educational Plan (IEP)   An individual programme for children with special needs.

makaton   A language-development programme using speech, signs and symbols for children and adults with learning difficulty.

one-to-one support   Working in a ratio of one adult to one child.

parent-partnership worker   A person who can support the parents of a child with disability in their dealings with the Local Education Authority.

portage   A home-based service for pre-school children with disability.

reception   The first year of infant education for children aged four to five years.

SATS   Standard Attainment Tests.

SEN   Special Educational Needs.

SENCO   Special Educational Needs Co-ordinator.

SLD   Severe Learning Difficulty.

statement   A statutory document that outlines the extra support or resources needed to educate a child with special needs.

year 1   The second year of infant education for children aged five to six years.

year 2   The third year of infant education for children aged six to seven years.

zimmie   The name given to Hannah's walking frame.

List of useful organisations

ADVISORY CENTRE FOR EDUCATION (ACE) provides information and advice on all aspects of state education. Has a handbook that deals in detail with the statementing procedure. *1b Aberdeen Studios, 22–24 Highbury Grove, London N5 2DQ. Tel no: 020 7354 8321.*

AFASIC association for all speech-impaired children. It organises activity week holidays for young people with speech and language disorders. *347 Central Market, Smithfield, London EC1A 9NH. Tel no: 020 7236 3632.*

CARERS NATIONAL ASSOCIATION provides information and campaigns for all carers. National advice line for carers: Monday to Friday 10.00 a.m. to 12.00 noon, 2.00 p.m. to 4.00 p.m. Tel no: 0345 573369. *20–25 Glasshouse Yard, London EC1A. Tel no: 020 7490 8818.*

COUNCIL FOR DISABLED CHILDREN provides advice on policies and good professional practice. *C/o National Children's Bureau, 8 Wakeley Street, London EC1V 7QE. Tel no: 020 7843 6000.*

DIAL UK is a network of 140 disability advice centres run by and for people with disabilities. *Park Lodge, St Catherine's Hospital, Tickhill Road, Doncaster DN4 8QN. Tel no: 01302 310123.*

DISABILITY ALLIANCE publish a disability rights handbook and have a rights advice line: Monday and Wednesday 2 p.m. to 4 p.m. 020 7247 8763.*Universal House, 88–94 Wentworth Street, London E1 7SA. Tel no: 020 7247 8776.*

DISABILITY LAW SERVICE *2nd Floor, High Holborn House, 52–53 High Holborn, London WC1V 6RL. Tel no: 020 7831 8031.*

DISABLED LIVING FOUNDATION gives expert and impartial advice about equipment for daily living. Help line: Monday to Friday 10 a.m. to 4 p.m. *Tel no: 0870 6039177. 380–384 Harrow Road, W9 2HU Tel no: 020 7289 6111.*

DOWN'S SYNDROME ASSOCIATION *155 Mitcham Road, London SW17 9PG. Tel no: 020 8682 4001.*

DOWN SYNDROME EDUCATIONAL TRUST exists to advance the development and education of children and adults with Down syndrome worldwide. *Sarah Duffen Centre, Belmont Street, Southsea, Hampshire PO5 1NA. Tel no: 01705 824261.*

FAMILY FUND TRUST is an independent organisation whose purpose is to ease the stress on families who care for very severely disabled children under 16. It provides grants and information. *PO Box 50, York YO1 9ZX. Tel no: 01904 621115.*

KIDSACTIVE (formerly HAPA) runs six adventure playgrounds in the London area for disabled children, children with special needs and their siblings and friends. It also offers training on the issues of inclusion of children of all abilities in play. *Pryor's Bank, Bishop's Park, Fulham, London SW6 3LA. Tel no: 020 7736 4443.*

INDEPENDENT PANEL FOR SPECIAL EDUCATION ADVICE (IPSEA) provides free and independent advice to parents of children with special needs including legal matters, second opinions on a child's learning difficulty and free support and representation for parents appealing to the Special Educational Needs Tribunal. Advice line: Monday to Thursday 10 a.m. to 4 p.m. and 7 p.m. to 9 p.m. *4, Ancient House Mews, Woodbridge, Suffolk IP12 1DH. Freephone 0800 018 4016.*

MENCAP National Centre for general enquiries and information. *123 Golden Lane, London EC1Y 0RT. Tel no: 020 7454 0454.* Early Years Project at Mencap London Division works with the families of children with learning disabilities so that they may enjoy the same rights, choices and opportunities as any other family. *115 Golden Lane, London EC1Y 0RT. Tel no: 020 7696 5581/6918.*

NATIONAL ASSOCIATION FOR SPECIAL EDUCATIONAL NEEDS (NASEN) aims to promote the development of children and young people with special educational needs. *Nasen House, 4 Amber Business Village, Amber Close, Tamworth B77 4RP. Tel no: 01827 311500.*

NETWORK 81 offers practical help and support to parents throughout all stages of assessment and statementing and gives guidelines on how to choose a school. It organises several befriender courses each year. *Tel no: 01279 647415.*

PEOPLE FIRST is a self-advocacy organisation run by and for people with learning disabilities. *Instrument House, 207–215 Kings Cross Road, London WC1X 9DB. Tel no: 020 7713 6400.*

PHAB promotes and encourages people with and without physical disability to come together on equal terms. It offers disability awareness training in primary schools and in corporations. *Summit House, Wandle Road, Croydon CR0 1DF. Tel no: 020 8667 9443. email* Phab@ukonline.co.uk.

SCOPE provides information and support to people with cerebral palsy, their family and carers. It also campaigns nationally and locally for equality for disabled people. *6 Market Road, London N7 9PW. Tel no: 020 7619 7100.*

SKILL National Bureau for Students with Disabilities promotes opportunities to empower young people and adults with any kind of disability to realise their potential in further and higher education, training and employment. *Chapter House, 18–20 Crucifix Lane, London SE1 3JW. Information line: 0800 328 5050 Monday to Friday 1.30 p.m. to 4.30 p.m. Main Tel no: 020 7450 0620.*

SPECIAL FAMILIES HOME SWAP REGISTER is a home exchange holiday service specifically deigned to cater for the needs of those with a physical disability, their families and carers. *Erme House, Station Road, Plympton, Plymouth, Devon PL7 3AU. Tel no: 01752 347577.*

Bibliography

Association of Teachers and Lecturers (1998) *Achievement for all*, ATL, London.

Beveridge, S. (1999) *Special Educational Needs in Schools*, 2nd edition, Routledge.

Department for Education (1993) *Education Act*, HMSO.

Department for Education (1994) *Code of Practice on the identification and assessment of special educational needs*, HMSO.

Department for Education and Employment (1997) *Excellence for All Children: meeting special educational needs*, HMSO.

Department for Education and Employment (1998) *Meeting Special Educational Needs: a programme of action*, HMSO.

Lorenz S (1998) *Children with Down's Syndrome*, David Fulton Publishers.

Lorenz S (1999) *Experiences of Inclusion: For children with Down's syndrome in the UK*, Down's Syndrome Association.

Walker M (1993) (Ed) *Makaton – National Curriculum Series Part 1*, The Makaton Vocabulary Development Project